MW00959408

A Concise History of the Jews

Also by Aeon History

Golden Laurels, Silver Seas: A Concise Survey of Greek History from the Bronze Age to the End of the Hellenistic Period

The Wolves of Mars: An Introductory History of Rome from the Rise of the Monarchy to the Fall of the Western Empire

The Introduction to Greek and Roman History Series: Golden Laurels, Silver Seas + The Wolves of Mars – Greek and Roman History from the Bronze Age to the Fall of the Western Roman Empire

and

Napoleon Unleashed: A History of the Revolutionary, Emperor, and Military Genius who Reshaped Europe and Defined Modern Leadership

Scan the code to see our full list!

A Concise History of the Jews

The People Who Wrestled with God, Ghettos, and Genocide to Achieve Modern Statehood

Aeon History

uxori liberisque

and

fratri parentibusque

Contents

Introduction

Amid today's geopolitical realities and persistent anti-Semitism, it's more important than ever to understand the history of the Jewish people. Whether you found your way to this title out of pure curiosity, or have a personal interest in Judeo-Christian religious history and theology—just by cracking open this book, you're well on your way to understanding how the Jews emerged from the Holy Land, and how the so-called "chosen people" thrive today.

Reading this book offers a concise, accessible guide through the winding paths of history and the place of the Jewish people in today's world. You'll gain insights into pivotal moments, from the ancient kingdoms of Israel and Judah to the horrors of the Holocaust and both the triumphs and missteps of the modern State of Israel as it continues to struggle to define its place within the greater context of the Middle East.

This book presents historical events in a slimmed-down, approachable way, avoiding the pitfalls of dense historical documentation in favor of an accurate yet concise narrative of some major areas of interest. Consider this book a quick primer to familiarize yourself with Jewish history and its facets, allowing you to understand the historical timeline of the Jewish people. The goal is to make a complex history approachable and easily understandable, providing a framework to appreciate the Jewish legacy and its continued relevance in today's world.

Of course, Jewish history and statehood are notoriously contentious issues. The purpose of Aeon History's *A Concise History of the Jews* is to present the arc of history as generally agreed upon by mainstream historians – a challenging enough proposition. Ancient history as a discipline yields too few facts for the modern reader, nor is it immune to modern attempts to lay claim to history for political purposes. And it would not be too far off to suggest that all modern history (as understood by the general readership) is propaganda – in effect, if not by design. Nevertheless, our intention is to inform and engage, not to convince.

As of this writing, the Israeli invasion of Gaza after the Hamas attacks of October 7, 2023, is ongoing. The international debate over how to address this latest flare-up of the Israeli-Palestinian conflict will surely continue for years. This book seeks neither to justify nor excuse any loss of human life. Rather, we will attempt to present what facts we can find and let the reader decide their opinions for themselves. We are under no illusions that complete success in this regard is possible; however, we press on in good faith to write a book as free of bias as possible. Any moral judgment that seeps through will do so because (we think) some events can shock the conscience even of the most dispassionate student of history.

Chapter 1: Beginnings in the Levant

The Levant is a region in the Eastern Mediterranean encompassing the modern-day states of Israel, Jordan, Syria, and Lebanon. It also includes the Palestinian territories, which Israel has occupied since 1948. This area, known for its diverse geography ranging from fertile plains to mountainous outcroppings, has been a crossroads of civilizations for thousands of years. The location and landscape of this crucial juncture between North Africa, the Arab Gulf States, and the Mediterranean have made it a coveted prize for empires and a historical melting pot of cultures, religions, and ideas over millennia. The Levant is where monotheistic religious practice first emerged. Thus, it is a region of great significance to adherents of Judeo-Christian and Muslim faiths worldwide.

This history of populations coming and going from the Levant, forced displacements, and the fact of its strategic value for empires and great rulers of the past make it a place where struggles over land rights are almost baked into the recipe. Like a complex layer cake, each substratum of the Levant's story reveals a new dimension of history, spiritual evolution, and geopolitical relevance. The nuanced history of the Levant helps frame our understanding of the emergence and enduring impact of Judaism within this historically rich and highly contested region.

The Bronze Age Canaanites (ca. 2,500-1,550 B.C.E.)

In the ancient Levant, during the Bronze Age, Canaanite civilizations thrived, and an early Semitic language believed to be similar to Hebrew first emerged. Canaanites engaged in trade with their Egyptian, Akkadian, Assyrian, and other neighbors and began forming city-states. In the early second millennium B.C.E., they began moving into the Nile Delta.

The Canaanites eventually took control of northern Egypt as the "Foreign Ruler," or Hyksos dynasty about 1650 B.C.E. – the fifteenth Egyptian dynasty. The Roman-era Jewish historian Josephus translated the term "Hyksos" as "Shepherd King."

Their archeological remains cluster in the north and east of the Nile Delta.

Around 1550 B.C.E., Egyptian rulers expelled the Hyksos people, forcing them to migrate from the banks of the Nile back to where they came from; the hills of the region that today encompasses Israel and Palestine. This group of "Shepherd King" Canaanite settlers laid the foundations of what later became known as Israel (The British Museum, n.d.).

This fertile environment up in the hills, nourished by the Mediterranean sun and enriched by the emerging distinct culture of these Canaanites expelled from Egypt, would later set the stage for the birth of a unique identity. But for this to happen, a new religion—Proto-Judeo Yawhism—would have to gain traction. This wouldn't happen for at least another 500 years.

Proto-Judeo Yawhism first emerged during the mid-Iron Age, as early as the 10th century B.C.E. (*Yahwism*, 2023). This marked a pivotal break from previous traditions, as some followers of *Yahweh* began to declare that there was only one god. By this point, the Paleo-Hebrew language was well-established, and by the 6th century B.C.E., biblical Hebrew was in its fully formed state (*Hebrew Language*, 2019).

Here, a distinct Hebrew identity began to emerge, influenced by the confluence of traditions, thoughts, and deep ties to the land. Thus, the ancient Levant served as the canvas upon which the story of the Jewish people was painted. It highlights their path, from ancient Canaanite ancestry to a unified nation, with a distinct narrative carved out in the hills above the Nile basin, stretching all the way to Jerusalem.

Early Israelite Archaeology

Archaeological evidence of the ancient Canaanites' migratory path to the Nile Delta dates back at least to 2000 B.C.E., when their donkey-driven caravans were pictured in Egyptian tomb paintings (The British Museum, n.d.). The first reference to Israel as a place is thought to be the *Merneptah Stele*, an engraved Egyptian monument from circa 1200 B.C.E. This stone carving, housed at the Egyptian Museum in Cairo, refers to a military action in historical Canaan, and contains hieroglyphs that are thought to spell out the name: Israel (*Merneptah Stele*, 2020).

Archaeological digs have uncovered 30 settlements dating back to the late Bronze Age (1500–1175 B.C.E.) and 250 settlements dating back to the period just after the start of the Iron Age (1175–1000 B.C.E.). These sites, which cover the hills of Israel and the occupied West Bank, stretch from the Jezreel Valley to the Beersheva Basin (Rendsburg, n.d.).

The well-known four-room house archetype, which some believe to be a characteristic feature of late Bronze Age Israelite settlements, was initially thought to be exclusive to these hill-country sites, and possibly exclusively built by Israelite tribes. Similar structures, however, have been found in the coastal plain and Transjordan, suggesting a wider use of this architectural style throughout this region. This means that houses such as these would have been built by other Semitic Levantine people who inhabited the low-lying areas of current-day Israel and Gaza, namely the Canaanite tribes that would eventually come to be called the Palestinians.

So, from a purely archeological perspective, there is nothing particularly "Israelite" about the architecture seen in the four-room house style typical of the region. Material remains rarely coincide precisely with linguistic, cultural, or national borders – archaeology is too imprecise a tool for social history. It's important to keep this in mind because the four-room house has been written about extensively by Christian Zionists as supposed proof of biblical narratives and claims to the land. However, the archeological digs that give us information on these ancient dwellings are best used to understand how people lived during this particular period, not to support assertions about primarily modern (and political) preoccupations.

What we should take a closer look at, however, is the evidence we have on the hill-dwelling Israelites and the movement of populations. Archaeological digs in the hills north of Jerusalem that have taken place since the 1970s confirm that there was likely a marked increase in settled Israelite populations around 1200 B.C.E., particularly in these highland areas (*Israelite Highland Settlement*, 2023). The increase in population found in these surveys didn't correspond with similar growth in the surrounding lowlands, however. These were likely inhabited by other Canaanite tribes, along with the *Philistines*, a migrant group from the Aegean.

Some scholars equate the Philistines to an offshoot of the mysterious "Sea Peoples," whose movements around the eastern Mediterranean basin reflect the tremendous social and demographic upheaval during the collapse of Bronze Age civilization. The Philistines inhabited the coastal region of the Levant during the transition from Bronze to Iron Age. Their territory centered around a five-city-state "pentapolis" in the region of Gaza. Their non-Semitic kingdom is a notable antagonist of the Israelites in their early literature. While the name "Palestine" (a Greek term) was derived from this group, the Philistines (an Aegean population) have no relation to the native Levantine people that much later came to be known as Palestinians.

The terminology and timeline is confusing, but the key takeaway from the archaeological record is that –

1. The Canaanite peoples of the Bronze Age Levant largely shared architectural styles, even if they started to diverge religiously, linguistically, and culturally in a large area of modern Syria, Lebanon, Israel, Palestine, and Sinai.

2. The southern Canaanite groups that invaded Egypt circa 1650 B.C.E. as the "Hyksos" returned and settled heavily in the highlands, particularly the hills north of Jerusalem. By 1,200 B.C.E., these may be identified with the earliest "Israelites," as attested in the *Merneptah Stele*. Many biblical scholars place David's United Kingdom of Israel around circa 1,050-950 B.C.E.

3. The Philistines were Greek or Cretan settlers in the lowlands of the Levant. They occupied lowland territory starting in the 12th century B.C.E., partially mixed with Canaanites, and remained an independent people until about the 7th or 6th century B.C.E.

4. In the Iron Age, the Canaanites continued to inhabit the area, evolving into several different groups, most notably the Phoenicians. These notable seafarers reached

their height in the 9th century B.C.E., founding colonies as far away as Carthage, in modern Tunisia.

Cultural and Religious Roots

The cultural and religious evolution of the Israelites during the early Iron Age is deeply rooted in the interconnected civilizations dispersed throughout the greater Middle East. This era, marked by advancements and interactions among societies, provided a fertile ground for the development of early Hebrew culture. Before we get too deep into the complex religious landscape of the ancient Near East and the specific practices within the Israelite and Judean traditions, it's important to first clarify who the Israelites and Judeans were.

The Israelites inhabited Canaan during a range of historical periods described in the Hebrew Bible when tribal civilizations ceded to a succession of monarchic dynasties. Their emergence in this region is often dated to the 12th century B.C.E. (see above), with their society and culture deeply influenced by the interactions and exchanges with the neighboring civilizations of Egypt, Mesopotamia, and the broader Levantine corridor (*Israelites*, 2024).

The term "Judean" refers to the inhabitants of the Kingdom of Judah; more specifically, the southern part of the region following the split of the united monarchy of Israel around the 10th century B.C.E. This division marked a political and territorial separation that led to varying religious practices and cultural developments distinctive to each kingdom.

The term "Hebrew" refers to both the language and the people associated with the early Israelites and Judeans, as well as their descendants. The Hebrew language is part of the Northwest Semitic language family, which also includes Phoenician and Aramaic. It's the language in which much of the Hebrew Bible, or Tanakh, was written. When we use the word "Hebrew," in many cases, we're also referring to the cultural traditions, practices, and developments associated with the people who spoke the language and inhabited the region of ancient Canaan, and later the kingdoms of Israel and Judah.

The religious practices of the Israelites and Judeans, while sharing a common heritage and cultural background, evolved distinctly over time, influenced by internal developments and external interactions. This evolution included the transition from a polytheistic practice, where multiple gods were worshipped, to henotheism, where one deity, Yahweh, received primary devotion amid a pantheon of other deities.

Emerging around the 10th century B.C.E., the Israelite and Judean religions initially embraced a form of polytheism common to the region (Wi. Brown, 2017). This religious framework included the worship of multiple deities, yet was characterized by a particular emphasis on one or two main gods—a practice known as henotheism. In the case of the Israelites and Judeans, this focus was predominantly on Yahweh (יהוה in Hebrew), who was regarded as the main deity amid the formation of these nascent states.

This inclination towards henotheism, and the eventual prioritization of Yahweh, can be traced back to the religious dynamics of the late Bronze Age. During this time, the interplay of various cultural and religious influences across the Middle East contributed to a religious landscape in which the worship of a primary deity coexisted with the acknowledgment of a broader pantheon of gods. As Israelite and Judean societies continued to evolve, so too did their religious practices, gradually moving from this initial polytheistic and henotheistic framework towards a more focused worship solely on Yahweh. This transition reflects both the unique socio-political context of these peoples and the broader patterns of religious change occurring throughout the region.

Religious Divergence Between Israelites and Canaanites

Initially, both the Israelites and Canaanites shared a common cultural and religious heritage, rooted in the broader traditions of the region. This shared background is evident in the polytheistic leanings of the early Israelite religion, mirroring the polytheism prevalent among the Canaanites, who worshipped various gods associated with natural forces and societal values. As the Israelite identity and religious expression evolved, departures from the Canaanite religion became increasingly pronounced.

The journey from polytheism to henotheism, and eventually to monotheism, is a defining characteristic of Israelite religious development. Unlike the Canaanites, the Israelites came to reject the existence of other gods in favor of an exclusive devotion to Yahweh, asserting his supremacy and singularity.

Another notable difference is seen in the representation of the divine. Canaanite religion made extensive use of idols and images to represent their deities, integrating these representations into their worship and rituals. Conversely, the Israelite religion evolved strict prohibitions against such physical depictions of Yahweh, emphasizing his transcendence and incomparability. This firm stance, free of idolatry, reflected a theological and philosophical assertion about the nature of Yahweh and the things he demanded of his followers.

The nature and focus of religious practices and rituals also marked a departure. Canaanite religion included rituals that the evolving Israelite faith came to view with disdain; most notably, cultic ritual prostitution (Fisher, 1976). This custom was common throughout ancient religion and appears in numerous mythologies, notably the Epic of Gilgamesh. Child sacrifice, however, remained an area of mutual interest for Canaanites, Israelites, and Judeaites. It was a common practice of the time that we first see challenged in the biblical narrative of

Abraham's offering of his son Isaac at the behest of Yahweh.

In the story of Abraham, we see the cultural divergence of the Israelites and Judeaites from this ritualistic slaughter associated with Canaanite religious practices. Yahweh sends a messenger who demands that Abraham untie his son on the altar. He lets him know that it was just a test to prove his faith, thus teaching the lesson that this type of sacrifice, while perhaps valuable in a symbolic sense, is no longer necessary. This is due to the changing tides of an emergent Hebrew culture informed by opposition to other peoples' (and its own former) practices.

Instead of continuing Canaanite practices, Israelites and Judeaites were beginning to sour on them, and they started to develop their own set of customs centered around animal sacrifices, purity laws, and festivals. This not only facilitated communal worship of Yahweh but also served to reinforce ethical and moral standards. These practices underscored a covenant relationship between Yahweh and the Israelite people rooted in mutual obligations and ethical living.

While the Canaanite religion was cultic and focused heavily on idolatry, fertility, the cycles of nature, and the prosperity of the community, the Israelite religion began to place a greater emphasis on ethics. The prophets that emerged within the religion championed themes of justice, righteousness, and the moral responsibilities of individuals and communities. This ethical focus became a hallmark of the Israelite faith, further differentiating it from Canaanite religious practices which were based more on paying tribute to the gods.

Patriarchs of the Hebrew Bible

As proto-Judeo Yawhism evolved and scribes began writing down the Hebrew Bible as early as the 8th century B.C.E., the stories of Abraham, Moses, King David, and King Solomon became foundational pillars in later Jewish tradition, each symbolizing key aspects of Jewish culture and religious identity. The narratives of these men, while still deeply rooted in the historical contexts of the time and the greater region, came to embody broader themes and values that became central to Judaism. This influenced the development of Christianity and Islam.

Abraham

Often referred to as the founding patriarch of the Israelites, Abraham instilled faith and obedience in Jewish tradition. His covenant with God marks the genesis of the Israelites as God's "chosen people," emphasizing the importance of steadfast, unwavering faith and a strict adherence to divine will. The relationship between Abraham and God is, in many ways, what lays the groundwork for Jewish identity. It reinforces the importance of commitment to God and the Jewish community's belief that they have a special standing among others.

Moses

Moses emphasizes the importance of law, leadership, and liberation in Hebrew traditions. His story, particularly the exodus from Egypt and the reception of the Torah, including the Ten Commandments, conveys the centrality of divine law in Jewish life. Moses' leadership in liberating the Israelites from bondage in Egypt and guiding them to a covenantal relationship with God reinforces themes of justice, adherence to divine commandments, and an enduring quest for freedom—all principles that are core to Jewish identity and value systems.

King David

The biblical figure of King David represents Jewish sovereignty and unity. His achievements, most notably uniting the tribes of Israel and establishing Jerusalem as the national and spiritual capital of the Israelites, are celebrated as epitomes of leadership and the desire for a unified nation of Hebrew peoples under God. David's story, especially his lineage, holds messianic significance in Judaism, with the expectation that if a Messiah figure ever emerges, they will come from the Davidic line.

King Solomon

King Solomon, the son and successor of David, is best known for his role in building the First Temple in Jerusalem. The First Temple became the focal point for Jewish practice, symbolizing God's presence among His people and serving as a tangible center of religious and national identity.

Before We Move On

As we wrap up our look into the origins of the first Jewish people, we already see an origin story that's rich with cultural and spiritual evolution. Our initial exploration invites us to further consider the impact of these historical narratives on contemporary understanding and perceptions of Jewish heritage. What we already see emerging is an emphasis on philosophical principles, moral codes, and ethics, values that have shaped Jewish history from its inception.

Looking forward along our historical timeline, we now find ourselves at the threshold of a new transformative era, one that's marked by trials and triumphs. In the next chapter, we'll take a look at the period of the Babylonian Captivity and the subsequent destruction of the First Temple—a time of great adversity that nonetheless helped ingrain a profound sense of resilience and adaptability within an emerging Hebrew identity.

Our exploration into these turbulent times and the exile that came from them doesn't just focus on the challenges faced, but also on finding the roots of the indomitable spirit that propelled the Jewish people through this era and laid the groundwork for the beliefs and practices that would stick with the tribe for millennia to come.

Chapter 2: Exile and Resilience

As developing philosophical principles, ethics, and values informed the Israelites, so too did the historical narratives of exile they faced. Through the smoke of a razed Jerusalem and the chains of captivity, a narrative of unyielding perseverance and faith was written, setting the stage for an extraordinary cultural and spiritual resurgence. The tale of the Jewish people in captivity and exile is one of transformation; of a people holding fast to their traditions while adapting to the unimaginable, and in doing so, laying the foundations for a continuity of deeply held principles and traditions.

Babylonian Captivity and the First Temple's Destruction

The historical context leading to the Babylonian captivity begins with rising tensions, and the subsequent dissolution of the joint kingdom of Judah and Israel, which was brought together under King David.

Whether the United Kingdom of Israel existed is part of an ongoing academic debate. However, archaeology supports widespread Israelite presence in the territories around Jerusalem. But even if David's unified Kingdom existed, it had split into two closely affiliated smaller Israelite kingdoms by about 900 B.C.E. Judah occupied the southern territory, with Jerusalem as its capital. Israel (also called Samaria) was to the north, and its capital may have moved, but seems to have been the city of Samaria by the end of this period.

The Kingdom of Israel, the northernmost part of the united monarchy, fell to the Assyrians in 722 B.C.E. The remaining part, the Kingdom of Judah, found itself caught between the emerging powers of Egypt and Babylon. This precarious position led to a series of political maneuvers, including alliances and rebellions, which ultimately drew the Neo-Babylonian Empire under King Nebuchadnezzar II into direct engagement.

The first significant escalation happened around 600 B.C.E., when Nebuchadnezzar decided to invade

Jerusalem, resulting in the deposition of King Jehoiachin. Jehoiachin, along with his court, family, and thousands of artisans and workers, were exiled to Babylonia, marking the beginning of the period known as the Babylonian captivity. This deportation wasn't just a political move; it was a strategic attempt to diminish the Kingdom of Judah's capacity to rebel by removing its leadership and scattering its population.

A decade into the conflict, the situation escalated following a rebellion against Babylonian rule. Nebuchadnezzar responded with a devastating siege of Jerusalem that destroyed the entire city, the Temple of Solomon included. This led to yet another, larger wave of deportations, deeply implanting the experience of exile into the collective memory of the Jewish people for the first of what would come to be many times throughout history.

The precise dates of the captivity are tough to pin down. While some scholars cite 597 B.C.E. as the date that the first of these deportations occurred, others negate the claim, saying that the narrative of King Jehoiachin along with his family and court being expelled isn't historically accurate and that the first deportation didn't happen until Nebuchadnezzar's destruction of Jerusalem in 586 B.C.E. If this were the case, this means that the Jews would have been held in Babylonian captivity for 48 years. From a biblical perspective, this period lasted 70 years. Some peg the dates at 608 B.C.E. to 538 B.C.E., others 586 B.C.E. to about 516 B.C.E.

The Temple's Destruction and Its Impact

The destruction of the First Temple was one of the most formative events in Jewish history. It wasn't just about the physical dismantling of a sacred architectural masterpiece—it was the fact that this marked the collapse of the Jewish state and the end of the Davidic monarchy and the united kingdom of Hebrew peoples he brought together. The Temple's destruction was a profound cultural and emotional shock to the Jewish people, shattering the foundations of their religious and communal life.

The First Temple wasn't just any place of worship to the Jews, either; it was the epicenter of Jewish spiritual life. It served as a gathering point for the kingdom's major religious festivals and served as a symbol of Yahweh's covenant with the Jewish people, making its destruction a spiritual catastrophe that left the community feeling abandoned and racked with grief. The loss of the Temple plunged the Jewish people, now under Babylonian captivity, into a profound crisis of faith and identity.

The emotional and cultural impact of this event is powerfully captured in the *Book of Lamentations*, traditionally ascribed to the Prophet Jeremiah and part of the Five *Megillot* (or Scrolls) of the Hebrew Bible. In the Christian Old Testament, it appears after the *Book of Jeremiah*. The book is a poignant expression of grief and mourning over the destruction of Jerusalem and the Temple, reflecting the depth of despair felt by the Jewish people.

The elegies found within its chapters articulate not just the physical devastation of the city and its holy structures, but also the social and spiritual disintegration that ensued. *Lamentations* became an integral part of Jewish liturgy, recited annually on *Tisha B'Av*, the day of fasting and worship marking the Temple's destruction, serving as a perennial reminder of the loss and a symbol of enduring hope for restoration.

The destruction of the First Temple also catalyzed changes in Jewish religious practice. With the central place of worship and sacrifice gone, the focus shifted toward studying the oral traditions that would become the *Torah*, the biblical source of Jewish law that encompasses the first five books of the Christian Old Testament: *Genesis, Exodus, Leviticus, Numbers,* and *Deuteronomy.* Moreover, they developed a greater emphasis on prayer and a more community-based religious life.

The cultural ramifications of the Temple's destruction extended beyond the immediate aftermath, influencing Jewish thought, art, and literature for centuries. It became a central motif in Jewish culture, cementing the hope for a future redemption in Jerusalem.

Life in Exile

Despite the challenges of living in a foreign land, the Jewish exiles in Babylonia demonstrated adaptability. They ensured the preservation of their religious and cultural heritage while also integrating some aspects of Babylonian culture into Jewish law.

One of the greatest transformations during the exile was the shift toward community-based religious practices, which were now a necessity. The temple's destruction meant that sacrificial worship was no longer possible. This fundamentally changed Jewish worship and rituals, as a greater emphasis on prayer, the study of the *Torah*, and the observance of religious laws became the norm.

The synagogue, smaller outposts for worship rather than the centralized Temple, became the place for communal worship and learning, laying a proto-foundation for Rabbinic Judaism, which would emerge in the 2nd century C.E. Synagogue-centered religious life still characterizes much of Jewish practice today.

The exile prompted the composition and transcription of Jewish texts, including parts of the *Torah*. The challenges of preserving Jewish identity and culture in a foreign land led to a concerted effort to document and codify Jewish oral traditions, laws, and historical narratives. This literary activity helped preserve the religious and cultural heritage of the Jewish people while providing a source of comfort and guidance through tough times. Scribing the words of what would become the *Torah* to vellum during this time helped further anchor the oral tradition and served to build a sense of continuity among the now diasporic population.

Despite their displacement, the Jewish exiles managed to maintain a distinct identity and adhere to their strict dietary laws, or *kashrut*. According to some biblical scholars, the observance of the Sabbath first emerged as a formal religious practice during this time (Livni, 2017). Both of these practices served as visible markers of the covenantal relationship Jews believed they had with God and served to distinguish them further from the Babylonians.

While they differentiated themselves through religious practice, the Jewish exiles were exposed to some new ideas, leading to some degree of cultural integration. The influence of Babylonian legal and administrative systems, for example, can be seen in some Jewish texts (Linfield, 1919).

The leadership of figures such as Ezra, Nehemiah, and Isaiah was what pulled the Jewish community out of the period of exile. Their efforts to rebuild Jerusalem and the Second Temple once released from captivity allowed the Jewish people to thrive once again in the Holy Land.

The Return to Jerusalem and the Second Temple

The Jewish captivity in Babylonia lasted until 538 B.C.E., when Babylonia was conquered by Cyrus the Great of Persia, who issued a decree that allowed the Jewish people to return to their homeland.

Not all Jews chose to return at this time; many remained in Babylonia, laying the foundations for one of the first major Jewish communities in the Diaspora: the Persian Jews. (Who would later, along with other Jews of the Middle East, Central Asia, and the Caucasus, come to be known as *Mizrahim*).

Of the exiled Jews, those who chose to return to the Holy Land faced the monumental task of rebuilding their society, including the reconstruction of the Temple in Jerusalem, which may have been completed as early as 516 B.C.E. Some Jewish texts, however, contradict this early date, having recorded the date as 350 B.C.E. (*Destruction of the Second Temple in 70 CE*, n.d.).

The return to Jerusalem, known as *Shivat Tzion* ("the Return to Zion"), demonstrated the enduring spirit of the Jewish people. Initiated by the Edict of Cyrus in 539 B.C.E., which directly preceded his conquest of Babylon, Jewish exiles could now reclaim their homeland and begin the arduous task of rebuilding their society from the ruins left in the wake of the Babylonian incursion. According to historical and biblical accounts, between 48 and 70 years had now passed since the exile began, and there was much rebuilding to do.

This return wasn't just about the physical transit back to these ancestral lands but rather came to symbolize a profound moment of renewal and hope for the Jewish people. The permission to return and rebuild Jerusalem and its Temple was a divine affirmation of their ongoing covenant with God. It represented a second chance to establish their religious and cultural identity in the Promised Land.

The construction of the Second Temple on the Temple Mount in Jerusalem was central to this process of communal and spiritual reconstruction. The Second Temple aimed to restore the splendor of Solomon's Temple, knowing that it would become a unifying symbol for the returned exiles; few of whom could have been alive when the First Temple was destroyed (according to the traditional chronology). Its completion, whether it occurred in 516 B.C.E., or later in 350 B.C.E., marked the end of the physical and spiritual exile, reinstating Jerusalem as the religious and cultural heart of Jewish life.

The Second Temple period saw several key developments in Jewish religious thought, including the emergence of various sects and the compilation of important texts that would later form part of the Hebrew Bible. This period in which Jewish life thrived, however, would fall apart some 600 years later at the hands of the Romans.

Key Archaeology from the Second Temple Period

Archaeological discoveries and excavations in Jerusalem offer us invaluable insights into the cultural and religious life of early Judaism. The findings allow us to frame biblical narratives within a real historical framework, revealing clues into the ancient beliefs, practices, and societal structures of the time.

The Dead Sea Scrolls

This ancient series of scrolls, discovered in archaeological digs from the late 1940s through the mid-1950s in caves near the Dead Sea, includes biblical manuscripts, sectarian writings, and apocryphal works. The documents help expand our understanding of Jewish theological thought and practice during the Second Temple period.

The Dead Sea Scrolls include the earliest extant copies of the Hebrew Bible, dating back to the 3rd century B.C.E., which provide revealing information on how the text was conceived of and disseminated in the middle of the Second Temple period. They also provide a window into the diversity of Jewish religious thought before the Christian era.

The sectarian documents, such as the Community Rule and the War Scroll, paint a picture of the beliefs and practices of a distinct Jewish group, possibly the Essenes (see below, Chapter 5), offering a glimpse into the variety of religious expressions within Judaism at the time. The Dead Sea Scrolls have thus been pivotal in broadening our understanding of the development of the Hebrew Bible and Jewish religious life during this period.

Excavations in Jerusalem

Excavations in the Holy City have unearthed artifacts and structures that testify to Jerusalem's long history as a religious and political center.

Notable discoveries include the remains of the Second Temple and the surrounding complex, such as the Southern Wall and the Pool of Siloam, which confirm the historical accounts of the Temple.

These findings corroborate biblical narratives while also providing researchers with a tangible connection to the ancient world, allowing us to better understand the daily lives, religious practices, and architectural achievements of the people who inhabited the region. Excavations have also revealed personal items, inscriptions, and remnants of homes and public buildings, which allow archeologists, anthropologists, and religious scholars to gain a better understanding of the culture and political dynamics of ancient Jerusalem.

Before We Move On

Looking ahead, we now find ourselves on the cusp of a new epoch in Jewish history. As the Persians under King Cyrus released the Jews from the Babylonians, the Israelites and Judeites were now charged with the difficult task of re-building and re-envisioning their place within the Holy Land.

The Second Temple was constructed on the Temple Mount, a place that much later in history was where Mohammed was said to have ascended on a winged horse. Today, it is home to the Al-Aqsa mosque and the Wailing Wall, the only remnant of the original Second Temple. The Wailing Wall is a place of pilgrimage for Jews all over the world, and the Al-Aqsa mosque has become a stage for attacks on Palestinians at the hands of Israelis, standing as a symbol of the enduring conflict between the two groups.

Cyrus' release of the Jews from Babylonia ushered in a new era of Persian rule, a period that would come to be marked by cultural exchange and the emergence of new dynamics in Jewish history. This era proved to be rich with cultural crossover and integration yet fraught with its own set of distinct challenges for the Jewish people. Despite the difficulties they faced, it was an era that further shaped the Jewish identity and religious practices in profound ways.

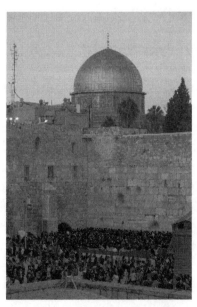

Chapter 3: Empires and Influence

Under the Persians, the Jewish people experienced a degree of autonomy that allowed them to rebuild their temple and re-establish their religious practices, albeit within the framework of a vast empire. Through the lens of history, we witness the remarkable adaptability of the Jewish people as they again navigated the complexities of life under foreign rule. The story of the Jews under Persian rule is one of enduring faith, cultural continuity, and the unyielding pursuit of autonomy, offering us lessons on the power of identity in the face of sweeping changes and powerful imperial forces.

Jewish Life Under Persian Rule

Under Persian rule, which spanned from the fall of Babylon in 539 B.C.E. up until the incursions of the Greeks under Alexander the Great in 331 B.C.E., Jewish life experienced a renaissance of sorts. This era, marked by relative autonomy under the oversight of the Persian Empire, witnessed shifts in both administrative and religious spheres for the Jewish community, while also preserving the essence of their traditions and beliefs.

Administrative Structures and Civic Continuity

The Persian Empire's administrative policies introduced a level of organization and stability not seen during the tumultuous years preceding Cyrus' conquest of Babylonia. By incorporating Judah, or *Yehud Medinata* as it came to be known within the vast Persian empire, the Persians allowed the Jews to self-govern under a system that collaborated effectively with the Persian imperial administration. Appointed governors (called satraps), such as Zerubbabel, a descendant of the House of David, and later Nehemiah, played pivotal roles in reinstating Jewish laws and rebuilding communal life in Jerusalem.

Religious Practices and Persian Influence

The focus of religious life at this time was the reconstruction of the Temple, which effectively re-established the centrality of worship and sacrifice in Jewish life. This act of rebuilding, underpinned by

Persian support, was emblematic of the Jewish community's enduring commitment to their faith and to maintaining a spiritual home within the Holy Land.

The influence of Persian Zoroastrianism during this period was reflected in the evolving Jewish religious thought, notably in concepts such as the belief in angels, the afterlife, and the battle between good and evil, concepts that may have informed later Jewish theological principles (Barr, 1985). The era was also an important one for the codification of Jewish law and the laying down of much of the textual foundation that would become the version of the *Torah* that we know today.

Cultural Integration and Language

Living under Persian rule, the Jewish people absorbed some aspects of Persian culture and religion. However, this integration didn't dilute their distinct identity. Instead, it showed the community's ability to maintain its core beliefs and practices amidst external influences. The preservation of the Sabbath, the abidance to the laws of *kashrut*, and the continuation of Hebrew as the sacred language of religious texts during this time attest to this enduring commitment to cultural heritage.

While Hebrew continued to be used for religious purposes and likely retained a significant role in daily life within the Jewish community, during this time, Aramaic was the *lingua franca* of the Persian

Empire, including the satrapy (or province) of *Yehud Medinata*. Aramaic's widespread use in the Holy Land was due to the administrative practices of the Persians, who adopted it as the official language of communication across their vast territory, which stretched from India all the way to Egypt. The adoption of Aramaic among the Jewish population was widespread, influencing how they conducted their administrative, legal, and even religious communications. Some portions of the *Torah* had sections that were originally written in Aramaic, reflecting its prevalent use during this time.

The Period of Greek Rule and Hellenistic Influence

The transition from Persian to Greek rule over the Jewish lands marked a shift in the region's historical and cultural landscape. This change was initiated by Alexander the Great's conquests, which, between 334 and 323 B.C.E., dismantled the Persian Empire and established Greek dominion over a vast territory, including the Levant. Alexander's campaigns spread Greek culture and language across the known world, ushering in the Hellenistic period, which would last until the rise of the Roman Empire.

The Impact of Greek Culture and Challenges to Jewish Identity

The introduction of Greek culture, or Hellenization of Judah, or *Judea*, as it became known under Greek rule, held deep implications for Jewish society. Greek city-states, or *poleis*, founded by Alexander and his successors, became centers of Greek language, arts, philosophy, and governance. This widespread cultural influence introduced Jewish communities to Greek philosophical thought and new forms of government and social organization.

For many Jews, the Hellenistic influence presented a challenge to their traditional way of life and religious practices. The emphasis on reason and humanism in Greek culture stood somewhat in contrast to the Jewish reliance on divine revelation and law. Additionally, the Greek practice of gymnasium education and athletic nudity conflicted with Jewish modesty laws and religious rites such as circumcision, showing how locker room anxiety existed even in the ancient world (Glick et al., 2022).

Jewish Response to Hellenization

The Jewish response to Hellenization wasn't monolithic, but rather tended to vary across different segments of the community. Some Jews embraced the Greek language and culture, seeing it as an opportunity for intellectual and social advancement. This led to the emergence of Hellenistic Judaism, which sought to blend Jewish religious traditions with Greek philosophical ideas.

However, the process of Hellenization also sparked resistance among those who viewed it as a threat to Jewish identity and religious observance. Tensions reached a boiling point with the policies of Antiochus IV Epiphanes, the king of the Seleucid Empire (one of the successor kingdoms of Alexander the Great's expansive Macedonian empire). He sought to aggressively impose Greek religion and culture upon the Jewish population. His desecration of the Second Temple and prohibition of Jewish religious practices, such as circumcision and Sabbath observance, ignited the Maccabean Revolt in 167 B.C.E.

The Maccabean Revolt and the Hasmonean Dynasty

Led by the priest Matthew and his sons, most notably Judah Maccabee, the Maccabean Revolt was a grassroots uprising against Seleucid rule and Hellenistic influence. The Maccabees' successful recapture of Jerusalem and rededication of the Second Temple in 164 B.C.E., celebrated annually as Hanukkah, the festival of lights, marked an important victory for Jewish autonomy and religious freedom.

The revolt laid the groundwork for the establishment of the Hasmonean dynasty, a period of Jewish independence and conquest. The dynasty was established by Simon Maccabee, the brother of Judah, and ruled Judea from 140 B.C.E. onward, marking the beginning of a period of Jewish independence. The Hasmoneans not only successfully threw off the yoke of the Seleucid empire, but also began to mount what became the only campaign to Judaize foreign populations in Jewish history with the forced conversion of the Idumeites, or Edomans (Berlin, 2011).

Judea experienced significant territorial expansion during this military and conversion campaign. John Hyrcanus I, Simon's son and successor, not only conquered Edom (or Idumea) but also Samaria and parts of Transjordan, incorporating these lands into the Jewish state. The Hasmonean dynasty lasted until 37 B.C.E., when the Romans appointed Herod the Great as King of Judea, effectively ending Hasmonean rule.

The Hasmoneans weren't just political leaders but also served as high priests, uniting both secular and religious authority in their hands. This dual role allowed them to oversee the Temple's religious functions and maintain Jerusalem's centrality in Jewish life. However, this combination of priestly and royal powers also led to internal conflicts and criticisms, particularly from the Pharisees (see below, Chapter 5), who opposed the Hasmoneans' interpretation of Jewish law and their use of force in religious conversions.

The period was marked by a flourishing Hebrew culture, with the patronage of arts and the construction of fortifications, palaces, and public buildings. The dynasty maintained complex relations with neighboring powers, including the Roman Republic, successfully navigating alliances and conflicts to preserve their independence. The treaty with Rome, established by Judah Maccabee and later renewed by his successors, was of particular strategic importance, as it offered Judea a powerful ally against ongoing Seleucid encroachments and later threats.

Despite their cohesive civic, religious, and cultural society, the Hasmonean dynasty was plagued by internal strife, including succession disputes and civil wars, which weakened their rule and made Judea vulnerable to external threats. The rivalry between the Pharisees and Sadducees, factions within Jewish society with differing views on religious and legal matters, further exacerbated these divisions.

Though the Hasmoneans considered Rome an ally, Rome eventually saw it necessary to intervene in

Judean affairs, so they installed Herod the Great as king, and eventually would fully annex Judea to gain more control. The dynasty's end marked the close of a unique chapter in Jewish history, characterized by a brief period of independence and significant contributions to the religious, cultural, and political development of the Jewish people.

Before We Move On

In the face of conquerors and conquests, Jewish people still demonstrated tenacity in maintaining their traditions and beliefs amidst the shifting sands of empire and the challenges of assimilation. As we close this chapter on the influences of empires and the remarkable saga of the Maccabees and the Hasmonean dynasty, we turn our gaze toward a new epoch marked by profound upheavals and enduring legacies.

The following chapter will examine the Jewish experience under Roman rule, a period that redefined Jewish history and set the stage for a larger and more enduring diaspora. This era came to be one that was fraught with challenge and change for the Jews as they witnessed the clash of mighty civilizations, the birth of pivotal movements, and the emergence of certain figures who would forever alter the course of Western and Near-Eastern monotheistic religious thought.

Chapter 4: Roman Dominance and the Diaspora

In 6 C.E., Judea's transformation into a Roman province marked the beginning of an era that would dramatically alter the course of Jewish history. This seemingly administrative change heralded a period of escalating tensions, culminating in widespread rebellion against the iron grip of Roman rule. The descent into chaos wasn't immediate, but the seeds of discord were sown early, as Roman dominance increasingly encroached upon the social, cultural, and religious fabric of Jewish society.

In this chapter, we explore the tumultuous period of Roman dominance over Judea, examining the impact of Roman rule on Jewish life. From the heroic yet ultimately tragic revolts that sought to reclaim Jewish independence to the catastrophic destruction of the Second Temple, we'll look at some of the events that reshaped Jewish society and set the scene for the early stages of the Jewish Diaspora that have endured up to the present day.

It's important to recognize that this time isn't just a story of yet another expulsion of the Jews from the Holy Land—we'll also be peering more deeply into the emergence of Rabbinic Judaism and how it evolved to maintain Jewish religion and cultural identity in the face of adversity and upheaval.

Jewish Life and Revolts Under Roman Rule

Under Roman rule, the social and political atmosphere in Judea was characterized by a complex interplay of resistance, accommodation, and escalating tensions that ultimately led to open rebellion. The Roman occupation formally began in 6 C.E., when Judea was annexed as a Roman province. The Romans introduced a series of administrative and fiscal changes that deeply impacted Jewish society.

The occupation imposed a level of control and influence that was unprecedented in its intensity and scope. Direct Roman administration brought heavy taxation, the appropriation of land, and the introduction of foreign customs and practices that clashed with deeply held Jewish beliefs and traditions. Against this backdrop of growing unrest, the Jewish people found themselves grappling with the challenges of preserving their identity and faith under the shadow of a powerful empire.

The taxes the Romans placed on agricultural lands, in particular, placed a heavy burden on the local population. The Roman practice of appointing and deposing high priests undermined the religious authority and autonomy of the Jewish community. The presence of Roman symbols and standards, viewed as idolatrous by devout Jews, further inflamed religious sensibilities and led to tensions between the occupier and the occupied.

The First Jewish Revolt (66–70 C.E.)

Roman rule was marked by a series of administrators whose heavy-handed governance and lack of sensitivity to Jewish customs and laws frequently led to friction. The Temple funds were being managed by a Roman treasury official named Gessius Florus, and the perceived mismanagement of these funds triggered the First Jewish Revolt. Frustrations stemming from oppressive taxation, legal injustices, and encroachment on Jewish religious life galvanized a broad spectrum of Jewish society against Roman authority.

These rising tensions finally led to an outburst after years of growing unrest in 66 C.E., when a series of skirmishes between Jewish groups and Roman soldiers escalated into a full-scale rebellion. The rebels quickly gained control of Jerusalem, expelling the Roman garrison from the city and declaring a new independence. The Roman response was swift and brutal.

In 67, Emperor Nero dispatched General Vespasian and his son Titus to suppress the rebellion. Nero is a notable antagonist in the Jewish tradition. He may have become the first persecutor of Christians, too, blaming them for the great fire that devastated Rome in 64. Of course, he likely considered them a fringe Jewish sect. Over the next few years, Roman forces reconquered the rebellious territory, culminating in the siege of Jerusalem in the year 70.

The period leading up to and even during the revolts was marked by internal divisions within Jewish society. Various factions, including the Pharisees, Sadducees, Zealots, and Sicarii, had differing views on how to respond to Roman rule, ranging from cooperation to heavy militant resistance. These internal conflicts often undermined the Jewish resistance effort and contributed to the revolt's ultimate failure.

The siege of Jerusalem ended with the destruction of the Second Temple, an event that, as with the First Temple's destruction, became a definitive moment for Jewish religious, cultural, and national life. The fall of Masada in 73 C.E., where the last of the rebels made a tragic stand, marked the end of the revolt. The aftermath saw the decimation of the Jewish population in Judea, the sale of many thousands into slavery, and the beginning of a more pronounced Jewish Diaspora as survivors fled Roman persecution.

The Destruction of the Second Temple and the Diaspora

The siege of Jerusalem was brutal and efficient. Starvation and disease decimated the defenders and civilian population alike. When the Romans, under the command of Titus, finally breached the city's defenses, they carried out a systematic campaign of destruction, which ended in the burning and looting of the Second Temple, the spiritual heart of Judaism.

The Temple was said to have been destroyed on the ninth day of the month of *Av*, the same Hebrew calendar date that Solomon's temple was said to have been destroyed almost 700 years before.

The destruction of the Second Temple wasn't just a military defeat, but a national and religious catastrophe that signaled the end of Jewish sovereignty in the Holy Land. The immediate aftermath of the Temple's destruction was devastating. The city of Jerusalem was largely razed, and the Jewish population was slaughtered, enslaved, or fled. The loss of the Temple, for the second time, left a void in the heart of Jewish religious life. Rituals and ceremonies that had centered on the Temple sacrifices were no longer possible, again necessitating a profound transformation in religious practice and community organization, as they'd done previously in Babylonia.

The long-term consequences of the Temple's destruction were even greater. The center of Jewish life shifted from Jerusalem to Jewish communities throughout the Roman Empire and beyond, marking the beginning of the Jewish Diaspora. This dispersion was not entirely new, as small Jewish communities had existed outside of Judea for centuries. However, the loss of the Temple as the unifying religious center called for the development of new forms of religious practice and community organization.

The immediate aftermath saw many Jews remain in Judea, continuing to live under increasingly oppressive Roman rule. However, the destruction also compelled substantial populations of Jews to seek refuge or establish new lives outside the Levant. Babylonia became a refuge for many, its Jewish community swelling with newcomers. This region, already steeped in Jewish scholarship and tradition from the earlier Babylonian Exile, became a vibrant center of learning, eventually giving rise to the Babylonian *Talmud*, one of the two versions of this holy book.

Egypt, and particularly Alexandria, with its pre-existing Jewish population, became another congregating point for the Diaspora. Here, Jewish thought and Hellenistic culture intermingled, perhaps best represented by the works of the Jewish philosopher Philo of Alexandria, who combined Jewish theology with Greek philosophy.

Further afield, in Asia Minor, Greece, and even in Rome itself, Jewish communities took root. In these places, Jews engaged in commerce, contributed to local economies, and established synagogues that served as places of worship and communal hubs, ensuring the continuity of Jewish life and practice. North Africa also saw the expansion of Jewish settlements during this time, particularly in the regions that comprise the modern-day states of Libya, Morocco, and Tunisia. These early Diasporic communities laid the foundations for a Jewish presence in North Africa that would endure for centuries.

The Diaspora wasn't just a story of dispersion, but one of profound adaptation and survival. Jewish communities, though now separated by vast distances, remained connected by a shared heritage and a commitment to their traditions. The development of Rabbinic Judaism during this time provided a religious and philosophical framework that allowed them to sustain their cultural and religious identity, no matter where they found themselves.

A new form of study, with an emphasis on law and moral codes, became the foundation of Jewish religious life in the Diaspora. The compilation of the *Mishnah* and later, the *Talmud,* codified Jewish law and tradition, ensuring the continuity of Jewish identity and practice across the dispersed communities.

The Development of Rabbinic Judaism

The emergence and evolution of Rabbinic Judaism in the aftermath of the Second Temple's destruction and the beginning of the Diaspora represents one of the greatest transformations in Jewish religious life witnessed up to this point. This period saw the transition from a religion centered around the Temple and its sacrificial cult to a more recognizable version of the faith (when seen through today's lens); this Judaism focused on *Torah* study, prayer, and adherence to *halacha* (Jewish law), practices that could be carried out in any place and under any circumstances.

Rabbinic Judaism has its roots in the Pharisaic movement, which emphasized the importance of oral law alongside the written *Torah*. The Pharisees believed that alongside the *Torah* given to Moses on Mount Sinai, an oral tradition interpreting and expanding on the written word was also transmitted. This oral tradition laid the groundwork for the formalized version of the religion that was to emerge.

After the Temple's destruction, the Jewish people faced a spiritual and existential crisis. Without the Temple as the central focus of Jewish religious life, there was a pressing need to redefine Jewish practice, and what it meant to be of the "chosen people." The leaders of the Rabbinic movement, successors to the Pharisees, rose to this challenge. They argued that true religious life shouldn't be confined to the Temple and its rituals, but rather, that it should be accessible to every Jew through the study of *Torah*, prayer, and the performance of *mitzvot* (commandments) as outlined in Jewish law.

Jewish Law: The **Mishnah** *and the* **Talmud**

The development of this new Judaism was characterized by the codification of the oral law. The *Mishnah*, compiled by Rabbi Judah the Prince around 200 C.E., was the first systematic collection of Jewish legal traditions, serving as a foundational anchor of Rabbinic Judaism. The legal discussions in this text were further elaborated in the *Gemara*, with the combined work known as the *Talmud* becoming the central text.

The *Talmud*, between its two versions, the Babylonian *Talmud* and the Jerusalem *Talmud*, includes centuries of rabbinical thought, debate, and interpretation. It covers not only legal but also ethical, theological, and practical aspects of Jewish religious life. The new emphasis on study and legal interpretation brought on by the adoption of the *Mishnah* and the *Talmud* enabled the Jewish people to maintain a sense of unity and continuity despite the physical destruction of their central religious site and the dispersion of the community.

The shift toward Jewish law also democratized religious practice, moving the focus from the priesthood and the Temple cult to individual and communal adherence to God's commandments as interpreted by the rabbis. This period saw the evolution of the figure of the rabbi, a teacher and interpreter of the law, who guided community matters that extended not just to the innately religious but also to deep moral and ethical questions.

Before We Move On

It's interesting to consider how the lines between the religious and the secular were navigated and often blurred during this historical period. In the wake of the Second Temple's destruction, the Jewish community faced a religious crisis first and foremost, but it also represented a profound socio-political upheaval that threatened to rupture the foundational elements of their society.

The rise of Rabbinic Judaism, however, marked a pivotal moment in Jewish history, bringing together religious practice, legal scholarship, and daily life into a cohesive picture that evolved into Jewish identity as we recognize it today. This era saw the rabbis taking on roles that went further than purely spiritual—they became community leaders, legal authorities, and educators, blurring the lines between the sacred and secular. In doing so, they crafted a version of Judaism that was deeply integrated into all aspects of life, making the religion more accessible and adaptable to dispersed people.

With the foundations of Rabbinic Judaism firmly laid and the Diaspora beginning to take shape under Roman rule, we now move to a new chapter of Jewish history. This next phase saw a continuation of the Jewish scholarly tradition cemented by the *Mishnah* and the *Talmud*, alongside the emergence of the various sects we've begun to look at, the Pharisees, the Sadducees, and the Essenes.

Chapter 5: Scholars and Sects

The Talmudic and Geonic periods comprise the pivotal centuries in which the *Mishnah* and *Talmud* were composed. In a world where empires rose and fell, the Jewish people persevered. Their traditions could often be maintained only through the transcription of Jewish law and practices.

Amid the shifting sands of Byzantine and Islamic rule between the 4th and 7th centuries C.E., Jews and the traditions they held continued to thrive. This was accomplished through continuous engagement with surrounding cultures while simultaneously carving out distinct religious and intellectual spaces that were exclusive to Jews.

This chapter looks at the emergence of influential sects like the Pharisees, Sadducees, and Essenes, each responding to the challenges of their time with unique visions of Jewish life and law. Their debates, struggles, and insights reflect the ever-questioning nature of Judaism, a religion constantly in flux, with both internal philosophical motivations and external pressures. As we peer into this era of great scholars and diverse sects, the complexity and depth of Jewish scholarly tradition emerge, allowing us to better appreciate how these centuries of change contributed to shaping a Jewish identity that is both ancient and ever-new.

The Pharisees, Sadducees, and

Essenes

From the Second Temple period (515 B.C.E.–70 C.E.) and up through the first few centuries of the Common Era, there was a profound political, social, and religious transformation within Jewish society. Three prominent sects emerged during this time: the Pharisees, the Sadducees, and the Essenes. Each group represented distinct philosophical and theological perspectives, and each contributed in its own way to Jewish thought and practice.

Pharisees

The Pharisees were a group of scholars and priests who were known for their emphasis on the oral tradition alongside the written *Torah*. They believed that in addition to the *Torah*, which was handed down by God to Moses on Mount Sinai, an oral law also had to be transmitted. This supplementary commentary interpreted and expanded upon the written word of the bible itself.

This emphasis on oral tradition informed the way the Pharisees approached Jewish law, which made them advocates for a more flexible interpretation that could adapt to changing times. The Pharisees were popular among the common people, partly because of their teaching that all Jews should strive to observe holiness in their daily lives.

The thoughts pioneered by the Pharisees continued to play an important role in the development of Rabbinic, and eventually Orthodox, Judaism in the wake of the Second Temple's destruction, and on into the 3rd century C.E. (The Editors of Encyclopedia Britannica, 2014a).

Sadducees

The Sadducees represented the interests of the priestly and aristocratic sectors of society, in contrast to the more populist, egalitarian Pharisees. Unlike the Pharisees, who emphasized oral traditions, the Sadducees adhered strictly to the written *Torah*. Within this sect, emphasis was placed on Temple rituals and sacrifices, and their religious authority was largely derived from their control of the Temple's functions.

This strict interpretation also extended to law, and the Sadducees were known for their harsh punishments for crimes. They believed strongly in *lex talionis*, the "eye for an eye, tooth for a tooth" doctrine (*Sadducee*, n.d.).

Though the Sadducees had an influential presence in the Temple and were essentially in control of it from at least the 2nd century B.C.E. onward, once the Second Temple was destroyed, the Sadducean influence began to wane (*Sadducee*, n.d.). They eventually disappeared as a distinct group.

Essenes

In contrast to the Pharisees and the Sadducees, the Essenes were a more ascetic and mystical sect, choosing to live in all-male monastic communities that were cordoned off from the larger Jewish society, and away from the looming presence of the Temple atop Temple Mount. Essenes didn't believe in Temple worship at all, instead choosing to observe their worship of the *Torah* independently.

The society they constructed was based on egalitarian principles, and private property was not allowed. The Sabbath was observed with rigorous day-long prayer sessions, and the rest of the week was spent toiling away at manual labor.

The group is often associated with the Qumran community, where the Dead Sea Scrolls were discovered. The scrolls provide insight into the Essenes' beliefs, which included immortality. They also believed that an apocalypse was to come in the form of a great war.

The Talmudic and Geonic Period

When Rabbi Judah the Prince, also known as Rabbi Judah the Patriarch, first sat down to undertake the monumental task of compiling the *Mishnah* around 200, he had quite a weight on his shoulders. Already, by the end of the 2nd century, the Jewish world found itself at a crossroads. The destruction of the Second Temple had left a vacuum in religious and communal life, challenging the continuity of Jewish tradition. On the cusp of the 3rd century, when Judah began to unroll his vellum, the

Jewish world was in desperate need of a text like the *Mishnah*.

The *Mishnah* was essentially an edited record of the oral *Torah*, an attempt to preserve the immense body of Jewish legal discourse that had been transmitted from generation to generation for centuries. By organizing these teachings into six orders covering various aspects of life and law, the *Mishnah* provided a structured approach to studying the oral traditions that accompanied the *Torah*, ensuring they would never be lost to time.

The compilation of these crucial traditions set the stage for the next phase of Jewish scholarship, leading to the creation of the *Talmud*. The *Talmud* was composed in two versions. The Jerusalem *Talmud*, the first version, was completed around the 4th century, followed by the Babylonian *Talmud*, which came together by the 6th century.

Both versions further elaborated on and discussed the *Mishnah's* teachings. Comprising the *Mishnah* as well as the *Gemara*—a later commentary on the *Mishnah*—the *Talmud* explores legal, ethical, and theological questions, reflecting the diverse viewpoints of rabbis over several generations. The Babylonian *Talmud* is notable for its breadth and depth, and it became the foundational basis of Rabbinic Judaism and an important record of Jewish life and thought.

The compilation of these texts occurred against a backdrop of political and social change. The Jewish community, now dispersed across the Roman and later Byzantine and Sassanian (or Second Persian) Empires, faced the challenge of maintaining a cohesive identity without a central temple or unified political leadership. The *Mishnah* and *Talmud* offered a way to unify Jewish practice and belief, providing a common framework for Jewish communities scattered across the known world.

These books were more than just legal codes, as they encapsulated the collective wisdom, ongoing debates, and intellectual rigor of the Jewish people. They offered guidance on everyday life, moral and ethical dilemmas, and the nature of the divine, making them central to the cultural and religious identity of the Jews wherever they found themselves.

Jewish Life in the Byzantine Empire and Islamic Caliphate

Jewish communities under the Byzantine Empire (313–636 C.E.) and Islamic Caliphate (638–1099 C.E.) experienced varying degrees of tolerance, pressure, and prosperity, navigating complex relationships with their rulers and non-Jewish neighbors. These interactions, often informed by the prevailing political, religious, and cultural climates, came to significantly inform Jewish life and practice.

Jewish Life in the Byzantine Empire (313–636 C.E.)

Under Byzantine rule, Jews found themselves in a Christian-dominated society that oscillated between tolerance and persecution. The early Byzantine period saw a continuation of Roman policies toward the Jews, including certain protections for Jewish practices. As Christianity solidified its grip on the empire, Jews often came to face more restrictive laws, forced conversions, and the destruction of synagogues, especially during periods of heightened religious fervor or when theological disputes brought Jewish belief systems into the spotlight.

Despite these challenges, Jews in the Byzantine Empire managed to maintain their unique religious identity, contributing to the economic life of the empire through trade, craftsmanship, and agriculture. The adversities they faced, paradoxically, fostered a strong sense of community and religious resilience, leading to achievements in religious scholarship, including commentary on the *Talmud* and the development of a set of Byzantine Jewish liturgical practices.

Jewish Life Under the Islamic Caliphate (638-1099 C.E.)

The advent of Islamic rule initially brought about a period of relative tolerance and prosperity for Jewish communities. Classified as "People of the Book," Jews, as well as Christians, were granted *dhimmi* status, which, while second-class, offered protections for their life, property, and freedom of worship in exchange for tax payments. This recognized status enabled Jewish communities to flourish, particularly in trade, medicine, and scholarship.

The Islamic Caliphates' expansive reach, from Spain to Persia, served to facilitate Jewish mobility and dissemination of ideas across an equally expansive cultural landscape. This led to a golden age of Jewish intellectual activity, particularly in the medieval period. The Jewish communities of *Al-Andalus* (Islamic Spain, today's autonomous community of Andalucía being the Hispanicized traditional Arabic name) are perhaps the most emblematic of this era.

In Spain, under Islamic rule, Jews made advancements in philosophy, poetry, and science and contributed to a transfer of knowledge that brought Greek and Roman ideas to the Arabic-speaking world. The interactions between Jewish communities and their Muslim and Christian neighbors during this period weren't just ones of coexistence, as there was much cultural crossover. In the Islamic world, Jewish, Christian, and Muslim scholars engaged in exchanges that enriched each other's intellectual and cultural heritage. Jewish philosophers like Maimonides were deeply influenced by Islamic philosophy, while Jewish mysticism was shaped in part by Islamic Sufism.

Before We Move On

The differences seen in the Pharisees, Sadducees, and Essenes during the Second Temple period and the centuries that followed offer us a fascinating glimpse into how Judaism developed. These sects, with their distinct beliefs and practices, laid a complex groundwork that, in many ways, informed the evolution of Rabbinic Judaism. The Pharisees' emphasis on oral tradition and adaptability, in particular, can be seen as a precursor to the Rabbinic movement that flourished after the Temple's destruction, guiding Jewish life through the principles that would become central to the Diaspora experience.

As we reflect on the contributions of these sects, it becomes clear that the richness of Jewish tradition owes much to the interplay of diverse perspectives and interpretations. Even centuries into the Diaspora, the echoes of their debates, the rigor of their scholarship, and their responses to the challenges of their times continue to influence Jewish thought and identity.

As we move forward from the era of great scholars and diverse sects, we enter a period marked by profound challenge and transformation. In the next chapter, we'll take a closer look at the lives and experiences of Jewish communities during the medieval period—a time characterized by remarkable achievements as well as some daunting tests.

We'll continue to look more specifically at how Jewish communities navigated the complexities of life under Christian and Islamic rule, contributing to the intellectual, cultural, and spiritual life that Jews continued to hold close to them throughout these times.

Chapter 6: Medieval Jewish Life

In an age that came to be characterized by both turmoil and enlightenment, Jewish communities across medieval Europe navigated a world of conflict, contrasts, and growth. From the shadowed veils of persecution to new heights reached in cultural and intellectual achievement, Jewish people in the Middle Ages again showed perseverance and adaptability, cementing a legacy of rich cultural life and continuing the preservation of the religious, moral, and ethical values they brought with them in the wake of the Temple's destruction.

This period, in general, was one in which Jewish communities faced several daunting challenges, including persecutions, expulsions, and the visceral tumult of the Crusades. Despite having the odds stacked against them by increasingly aggressive Christendom, the Jewish people experienced periods of remarkable flourishing, most notably under the protection afforded to them in Islamic-ruled Spain, or *Al-Andalus.*

As we further explore the diverse experiences of Jewish communities, from the cobblestone streets of medieval Europe to the scholarly halls of the Islamic world, we uncover a story of intellectual heights reached and the harrowing depths of persecution that have historically plagued the Jewish people.

Jewish Communities in Medieval Europe

Throughout the medieval period, Jewish communities in Europe experienced a wide range of living conditions and filled varying societal roles, each being influenced by the wider religious, economic, and political contexts of the time. One of the starkest contrasts is seen in their treatment in Christian Europe versus in the Iberian Peninsula under Islamic rule.

The Jews in Medieval Europe

In the Mediterranean

The transplantation of Jewish life from the Levant to the Greater Mediterranean after the Second Temple's destruction eventually took the Jewish people to the farthest reaches of the Roman Empire. Centuries later, they began to migrate to parts of Eastern Europe well outside the bounds of the successive Byzantine and Holy Roman Empires.

In the direct aftermath of the Second Temple's destruction, one early destination for newly Diasporic Jewish communities was Rome itself, where they were met with both tolerance and persecution. In Rome, Jewish communities established themselves first in Trastevere (across the river) and Tiber Island.

Roman Jews contributed to local economies and engaged in cultural exchanges, despite facing some restrictions and periodic violence once the Edict of Thessalonica in 380 C.E. made Christianity the official religion of the Empire. The Jews of Rome maintained a continuous presence in Rome from antiquity through the Middle Ages and were later ghettoized on the opposing bank of the Tiber, where the main synagogue and Jewish Ghetto still stand today.

Migration Into Central Europe

The Jewish presence in Central Europe, particularly in areas that would later become part of the Holy Roman Empire, marked another chapter in the Diaspora's progression. Jewish communities began to settle in the Rhineland and other parts of Central Europe during the early Middle Ages, often invited by feudal rulers who valued their economic contributions, especially in trade and finance. Cities like Worms and Trier, in what is now Germany's Rhineland, and Metz, in France, became vibrant centers of Jewish life.

However, this period was also marked by hardship. The First Crusade in 1096 devastated many of these early communities. Subsequent crusades and local conflicts often resulted in persecution and expulsion, pushing Jewish populations further into Eastern Europe and creating new centers of Jewish life in what was then the Kingdom of Poland and Lithuania (later to become part of the Austro-Hungarian Empire), where they would again contribute to the local economies and cultural life.

In Christian Europe, Jews faced a paradox of essential economic roles and systemic exclusion. Christian usury laws banned money lending between Christians, and this relegated Jews to finance-related occupations, a necessity for local economies but also a source of resentment and scapegoating.

Periods of tolerance were punctuated by intense persecution, including the first pogroms, expulsions, and forced conversions, notably during the Crusades and during the Bubonic Plague, when Jews were falsely accused of having something to do with the mass wave of sickness and death that swept Europe from 1346 to 1353.

Throughout the medieval period in Europe, Jewish communities managed to preserve their traditions and identity while navigating the often hostile societies in which they lived. The Jews' presence in Central Europe throughout the Middle Ages laid the groundwork for future generations and for the emergence of the Yiddish language and a distinct Ashkenazi culture throughout Central Europe, which later moved into the Eastern European Regions of Galicia, and the Pale of the Settlement.

The Jews in Al-Andalus (Islamic Spain)

The saga of the Jews in *Al-Andalus* represents a unique chapter in Jewish history, marked by unprecedented levels of cultural, intellectual, and religious exchange. From the 8th to the 15th centuries, under Muslim rule, Jews in the Iberian Peninsula experienced a period of relative tolerance and integration, contrasting sharply with what Jews in Christian Europe experienced.

As mentioned in the previous chapter, upon the Islamic conquest of Spain in 711, Jews were granted special status as *dhimmis*. This designation meant that they could continue to practice their religion in exchange for a tax. The status afforded Jewish communities a degree of protection and autonomy that was unheard of in many other parts of medieval Europe.

The establishment of *Al-Andalus* as a center of Islamic culture helped usher in what's often referred to as the Golden Age for Jewish life and scholarship. In cities like Córdoba, Granada, and Seville, Jewish intellectuals thrived, contributing to the fields of philosophy, medicine, poetry, and science. This era was emblematic of a culture of *convivencia*, or coexistence, where Muslims, Christians, and Jews shared knowledge, culture, and even language, leading to a rich cross-fertilization of ideas.

Jewish philosophy flourished remarkably during this period, as Jews living under the Islamic Caliphate explored the intersection of faith, reason, and ethics. One of the most prominent figures to arise from Spain's Golden Age was Moses Maimonides (1135–1204), a philosopher, rabbi, and physician whose work, *Guide for the Perplexed,* explores the connections between religion and philosophy.

Jews also played an important role in the field of medicine, both as practitioners and scholars. Maimonides again stands out here as a main contributor. His body of work includes numerous texts on health, diseases, and treatments that were centuries ahead of their time. During these times, highly esteemed Jewish physicians in *Al-Andalus* were frequently sought after by kings and caliphs. The writings of these doctors, which included translations of Greek and Arabic medical texts into Hebrew and Latin, helped transmit medical knowledge across cultural boundaries, accelerating the development of scientific medical knowledge in Europe.

In the literary arts, Jewish writers contributed to the preservation and development of Jewish culture and identity. Poetry from Spain's Jewish Golden Age, for instance, saw figures like Judah Halevi and Solomon ibn Gabirol blend religious devotion with artistic personal expression, presenting a mix of Hebrew literary traditions with those of the Islamic world. Jewish storytelling, embodied in collections like Joseph Zabara's *The Book of Delight*, provided both entertainment and moral and philosophical insights.

The intellectual and cultural achievements of Jewish communities in Iberia during this transitional historical period had a lasting impact on global knowledge. Through their scholarly pursuits, Jewish thinkers helped preserve the intellectual heritage of the ancient world while contributing to the advancement of sciences and humanities. Their works facilitated cross-cultural exchanges, particularly in the translation movements that brought Arabic and Greek knowledge to the Christian West, knowledge that would later fuel the European Renaissance.

This period of relative peace and intellectual flowering did not come without its challenges. The status of Jews as *dhimmis* meant that their rights and safety could be, and were, periodically undermined by political and social upheavals. The Almohad Conquest of the 12th century, for example, imposed stricter interpretations of Islamic law, leading to persecutions and forced conversions of Jewish communities. This prompted many Jews to flee to the Christian North or across the Mediterranean to Italy, Greece, and beyond.

Despite these challenges, the legacy that the Jews carved out in *Al-Andalus* under Islamic rule remains a strong example of the kind of cultural and intellectual symbiosis that Jews have been able to achieve wherever they've found themselves across the world. It serves as a reminder that there were places, even in the so-called "Dark Ages," where religious and cultural boundaries were more permeable. This allowed for a remarkable period of Jewish cultural and intellectual achievement that would influence the broader Mediterranean world and beyond.

As the *Reconquista* mounted, Christian kingdoms from the North began to reclaim Iberian territory from Muslim rule. The situation for Jews in the Peninsula would change dramatically with this shift, eventually culminating in the Inquisition and the expulsion of 1492. Yet, despite the threats posed by the Christian North, the developments pioneered by Jewish scholars, poets, and thinkers during the Islamic period in Spain would continue to be important for centuries to come, shaping the course of Jewish and world history in profound ways.

Spain's Golden Age Comes to an End

During the medieval period, Jewish communities in Europe faced a broad array of challenges, from the Crusades to widespread expulsions; yet, they also experienced periods of remarkable cultural and intellectual flourishing. This duality of experience again demonstrates the resilience and adaptability Jews continued to demonstrate in the face of adversity during these testing and traumatic times.

The Crusades

Jewish history during the medieval period is marked by a series of deeply traumatic events that had lasting impacts on Jewish communities across Europe. This era was characterized by widespread violence, forced conversions, and the uprooting of entire communities, often under the banner of religious fervor and empire expansion.

The first crusades, which were mounted at the end of the 11th century, were primarily aimed at reclaiming Jerusalem and the Holy Land from Muslim control. However, these military campaigns abroad also unleashed a wave of anti-Semitic violence in Europe.

The First Crusade (1096–1099), in particular, saw horrifying massacres of Jewish communities in the Rhineland cities of Worms, Mainz, and Cologne, places where Jews had settled and thrived. Crusaders, motivated by a combination of faith-inspired zeal, a desire for wealth, and the Papal promise of absolution for sins, attacked Jewish settlements, in many cases offering conversion to Christianity as the only alternative to death. Subsequent Crusades rippled throughout Europe and continued to pose threats to Jews, both directly through violence and indirectly through the heightened climate of religious intolerance they engendered.

In England, the blood libel accusation first emerged in the 12th century, asserting that Jews routinely murdered Christians to use their blood in religious rites. This lead to massacres and increased suspicion towards Jews. In France, Jews were periodically expelled, most notably in 1306 and 1394, and weren't allowed to return until the French Revolution in the late 18th century.

The Shepherds' Crusades of 1251 and 1320, though lesser known, had already been particularly devastating for Jewish communities in France. These crusades were led by groups of peasants who, inspired by the same religious fervor that fueled the larger Crusades, targeted Jews. In the case of the latter attack of 1320, Jews were targeted for their links to monarchs and their roles as moneylenders and tax collectors (*Shepherds' Crusade 1320*, 2024).

The patterns of rural violence against Jewish communities would continue to be seen well into the 19th and 20th centuries in Eastern Europe. *Pogroms*, localized instances of shocking violence where Christians would engage in round-ups and mass executions of their Jewish neighbors, became more frequent.

The Crusades deeply affected the Jewish psyche, leading to a profound sense of vulnerability. This prompted new waves of Jewish migration, particularly deeper into Eastern Europe, where Jews hoped to find a respite from persecution, only to find it yet again upon resettlement.

This period highlights the precarious position of Jews in medieval Europe, caught between their roles as integral members of the economic and social fabric of their respective societies and as perpetual outsiders. The widespread persecution not only decimated populations and displaced communities but also reshaped the Jewish Diaspora, setting the stage for the development of new centers of Jewish life in Eastern Europe and the Ottoman Empire.

The Demise of Spain's Golden Age: The Reconquista

The Golden Age of Jewish culture in Spain, between the 9th and 12th centuries, saw remarkable achievements in poetry, philosophy, and science. However, as the political and religious landscapes evolved, the prosperity and intercultural harmony of this period began to diminish.

The decline of this era, in which Jewish life and culture flourished, was fueled by several key factors. The fragmentation of the Caliphate of Córdoba in the 11th century led to the emergence of smaller, less stable Taifa kingdoms, leaving Jewish communities more exposed to the changing inclinations of rulers and diminishing their ability to secure the protections once afforded under unified Islamic governance.

The entry of the Almoravids and, later, the Almohads from North Africa introduced a more dogmatic interpretation of Islam to *Al-Andalus*. The Almohads, in particular, exhibited a stark intolerance for religious pluralism, compelling both Jews and Christians in *Al-Andalus* to convert to Islam under threats of persecution or death.

As these movements spread, the Christian *Reconquista* of Muslim-held territories swept in and introduced new power dynamics and conflicting religious fervor to the region. While some Jewish communities initially thrived under re-established Christian rule, the unification of Christian kingdoms throughout Europe, including in Iberia, often led to increased levels of religious intolerance and restrictions on Jewish practices.

Economic envy further exacerbated tensions, as Jews' prominent roles in administration, medicine, and commerce sometimes incited resentment among the Christian and Christianized populace of reconquered Iberia. This was particularly pronounced during times of famine, plague, and economic hardship, where Jews continued to be scapegoated.

Despite periods of notable intercultural exchange under re-established Christian rule, Jews in Spain and Portugal often found themselves socially and religiously segregated, more and more living in distinct quarters and adhering to unique customs. This separation, while preserving Jewish identity, also rendered Jewish communities more susceptible to targeting and marginalization during periods of turmoil.

The decline of Jewish life and culture in the Iberian Peninsula signified the loss of a homeland for Diaspora Jews who had established themselves there. It also marked a shift in Jewish intellectual, cultural, and religious life. The dispersal of Spanish and Portuguese Jewry catalyzed the spread of "Sephardic" (derived from the Hebrew for Spain: "Sefarad") culture and traditions across the Mediterranean and the Ottoman Empire, impacting Jewish communities far beyond the Iberian Peninsula.

The enduring legacy of Spain's Golden Age, however, demonstrates the potential for cross-cultural exchange and intellectual achievement. It continues to inspire and shape Jewish thought and identity to this day, underscoring an important chapter in Jewish and (specifically) Sephardic cultural history.

By the time the Middle Ages were coming to a close, new threats were at hand. Rather than being praised for their contributions to the arts, culture, and sciences, the Jews were once again threatened by a new crusade mounted by the monarchs of Spain.

The Spanish Inquisition

The Inquisition was a series of measures designed to uphold Christian religious principles and forcibly impose them on those who didn't conform. It was put into place by the monarchs of the Kingdoms of Aragon and Castile, Ferdinand II and Isabella I, in 1478. This marked a turning point in the history of Spain's Jewish and *converso* (Christianized Jewish) populations and signified a distinct end to the Middle Ages and the flourishing of the Jews in Iberia.

Ostensibly created to enforce Catholic orthodoxy and root out heresy, the Inquisition quickly focused its efforts on the *conversos*, suspecting them of crypto-Judeo religious practice. This period of intense scrutiny, persecution, and forced conformity had profound and tragic consequences for Jewish life in Spain, leading to the Alhambra Decree of 1492, which expelled practicing Jews from Spanish territories.

The Inquisition employed severe methods, including torture, burnings, and other forms of public executions, all designed to force them into confessions of heresy. Thousands of *conversos* were tried, and many were executed or faced severe penalties, including confiscation of property. The atmosphere of fear and suspicion eroded the fabric of community life, forcing many Jews to flee or convert to Christianity, while others practiced their faith in secret at great personal risk.

Before We Move On

The transition from Spain's Golden Age, a period marked by unprecedented cultural and intellectual achievements under a canopy of coexistence, to a time of severe persecution poignantly reflects on the cyclical nature of history as it affects the Jewish people.

The stark shift from progress, stability, and cultural flourishing to widespread expulsion and inquisition prompts us to consider the fragile balance between tolerance and intolerance that the Jews have historically faced. This pattern is one that, lamentably, has been repeated throughout Jewish history: Moments of cultural and intellectual contribution and integration followed by periods of persecution and expulsion.

In the coming chapters, we'll be looking at how Jews navigated the Renaissance, Reformation, and Enlightenment—periods that promised a fresh landscape for Jewish communities to continue their preservation of traditions and the development of new cultural modes. These eras brought about significant shifts in thought, society, and power structures, offering Jewish communities new avenues to contribute to the world around them. Yet, once again, they also brought forth a new set of challenges, as the enduring cycles of acceptance and persecution continued to unfold into the Renaissance and beyond.

Chapter 7: Renaissance, Reformation, and Enlightenment

Picture a world on the brink of profound change; one where the very foundations of society, belief, and knowledge are constantly questioned and redefined. The period from the Renaissance, up through the Reformation and Enlightenment came to be one of unparalleled intellectual, cultural, and spiritual upheaval for the Jewish people. After the intellectual dearth of the Dark Ages, a new spirit was born, and for the Jews, this represented both opportunities and challenges.

These eras weren't just historical backdrops that Jewish life played out upon but were rather obstacle courses of sorts. During this time the Jews made numerous contributions to burgeoning fields of knowledge. They also sought to carve out a place as dynamic, moral leaders and thinkers in rapidly changing societies. Instead of being met with praise, they were often targeted. This chapter is about how Jewish life was reshaped during these times, highlighting the struggle for emancipation, the blossoming of cultural and intellectual pursuits, and the profound shifts in Jewish thought and identity.

For Jewish communities on the brink of great cultural shifts, there were many looming questions to confront. How did they navigate this whirlwind of change? How did they find their place within societies that were simultaneously opening up to new ideas while grappling with deep-seated prejudices?

Through the lens of these pivotal periods, we'll take a closer look at how Jewish thinkers, artists, and leaders engaged with and, at times, came up against the broader movements of their time. They contributed to Europe's cultural and intellectual heritage while navigating the complex realities of their status as Jews. From the ghettos of Venice to the intellectual salons of Enlightenment Europe, Jewish communities left an indelible mark on the era, influencing and being influenced by the sweeping changes of the time.

Renaissance and Reformation Communities

The Renaissance and Reformation periods saw a series of transformations ripple across Europe, reshaping the continent's intellectual, cultural, and religious landscapes. For Jewish communities, though they were still relegated to specific societal roles and forms of work, these times were deeply transformative. Amid all the residual persecution and pigeonholing that the Dark Ages left behind, some newfound opportunities emerged, and an enduring candle of hope continued to shine.

The Renaissance in Italy

The rebirth of art, science, and literature across Europe ushered in by the Renaissance saw Jews making contributions, albeit often from the margins of society. In Italy especially, Jewish intellectuals, artists, and financiers played integral roles in society. Italian-Jewish thinkers, such as the geographer and scribe Abraham Farissol, engaged with the wider intellectual currents, writing on topics as diverse as New World discoveries, the celestial realm, and Jewish thought. The German-born Jewish scholar Elijah Levita became instrumental in the study and teaching of Hebrew in Venice. Though Levita's family had been deported from Germany for being Jewish, there was much cross-cultural exchange between the Jewish and Christian worlds in Italy.

In science and medicine, Jews' contributions continued to be highly valued. Jewish physicians, often educated in the most prestigious medical schools of Italy, were highly sought after. Their scholarly contributions to medical literature, including commentaries on the ancient physicians Galen and Hippocrates, along with original works, helped transmit and expand medical knowledge throughout Europe.

In the world of finance, Jewish bankers and money lenders continued to be scapegoated as they continued the medieval tradition of loaning to Christians, facilitating the growing commerce of the era. Jewish financiers served as vital cogs in the economic machinery of Renaissance city-states and kingdoms. They were forever immortalized, though often stereotyped through popular fictional portrayals, such as the character Shylock from Shakespeare's *The Merchant of Venice*. Their expertise in languages and international connections also made them indispensable as intermediaries in the trade of goods, from textiles to spices.

Artistically, Jewish craftsmen and artists contributed to the flourishing culture of the time, despite facing restrictions on their public expression and participation in guilds. Jewish craftsmen and artists made impactful contributions to the Renaissance's blossoming art movements. Italian-Jewish artists like Bonaiuto de' Pitati and Daniel da Volterra were active during this period, although their Jewish identity is often overlooked in historical accounts. The production of beautifully illuminated Hebrew manuscripts and the decoration of synagogues in the Renaissance style further attest to the artistic contributions of Jews during this period.

Additionally, the printing revolution of the 15th century saw Jews at the forefront of publishing Hebrew texts, spreading Jewish thought and religious texts more widely than ever before. The Milanese Soncino family, for example, were pioneers in printing the *Talmud* and other Jewish texts, greatly facilitating the spread of Jewish learning and thought. This innovation helped democratize access to Jewish scholarship while preserving Jewish culture and religious practices.

Though the social and cultural status of Jews during the Renaissance varied widely across Europe, in the Italian city-states, Jews found a degree of tolerance and could engage in commerce and intellectual pursuits, albeit within the boundaries imposed on them.

The First Jewish Ghettos

The Renaissance marked a turning point in the social organization of Jewish life with the establishment of the first Jewish ghettos. The term "ghetto" originally referred to the foundry district in Venice, Italy, but it came to denote the segregated quarters where Jews were forced to live from the 16th century onward. The creation of these ghettos was a paradoxical development during a time celebrated for its advancements in arts, science, and humanism.

In 1516, the Venetian Republic decreed the establishment of the Venice Ghetto, the world's first ghetto, to isolate Jews from the Christian population. This confinement was justified by the state for various reasons, including religious prejudice, economic envy, and social control. The Venice Ghetto wasn't just a place of segregation, but also of intense surveillance and restriction on Jews' movements, with gates that were locked at night.

Despite the oppressive conditions, the ghettos became centers of Jewish life and culture. Confined to these cramped spaces, and only limited to certain forms of work, Jewish communities managed to cultivate a rich cultural life, establishing synagogues, schools, libraries, and printing presses that made the ghettos vibrant centers of Jewish learning and spirituality. The Venetian Ghetto, in particular, became a hub for Hebrew printing, contributing significantly to the preservation and dissemination of Jewish texts and knowledge.

The establishment of ghettos spread to other parts of Italy and beyond, becoming a common feature of Jewish life in Renaissance Europe. In Rome, Pope Paul IV ordered the creation of the Roman Ghetto in 1555, imposing even harsher restrictions on the Jewish community, including the requirement to wear specific yellow garb when traversing through other parts of the city. Similarly, ghettos were eventually established in Central European cities such as Frankfurt and Prague, each with its own regulations and degrees of severity in terms of confinement and discrimination.

Within these confined quarters, Jewish life still flourished, albeit under these highly taxing and unfair conditions. The ghettos, in some ways, served as incubators for maintaining Jewish identity, traditions, and cultural achievements during a period when external pressures sought to diminish or erase Jewish presence from the European landscape.

This development reflected the broader contradictions of the Renaissance period, where the pursuit of humanist ideals existed alongside entrenched prejudices and systemic exclusion. The ghettos, while symbolizing the isolation and persecution faced by Jews, also represented their enduring spirit and capacity to nurture community, culture, and faith under the shadow of adversity.

Reformation

The Protestant Reformation, the movement that followed Martin Luther's *95 Theses* of 1517, marked yet another shift in Europe's religious landscape. It challenged the hegemony of the Catholic church and led to the establishment of Protestant churches. This period of religious transformation had profound implications for Jewish communities.

For the Jews, the Reformation somewhat represented a double-edged sword. On one hand, the questioning of Catholic orthodoxy opened new dialogues between Jews and Christians, with some Reformers advocating for a more humane treatment of Jews, seen as potential allies against a common Papal adversary. On the other hand, the period also saw an intensification of anti-Jewish rhetoric, including from Luther himself, who, despite an initial openness, later espoused virulent anti-Jewish views.

Some Protestant Reformers were attracted by the idea of returning Christianity to its "Hebrew roots," and sought to learn Hebrew and engage with Jewish scholars to better understand the *Old Testament* in its original language. This intellectual curiosity led to a somewhat improved relationship between certain Protestant groups and Jews, with figures like Philipp Melanchthon showing a more respectful attitude towards Jewish scholarship. But overall, Jews were frowned upon by the movement.

In his 1543 work, *On the Jews and Their Lies*, Luther espoused vehemently anti-Jewish rhetoric, advocating for their expulsion from Christian lands and the destruction of their synagogues and books. This work would, unfortunately, lay the groundwork for centuries of anti-Semitic thought and policy in Protestant countries.

The somewhat varied, but overall harshly negative sentiment toward Jews expressed by Protestants during the Reformation era, reflects the theological complexity of this radical reorientation in Christianity. In some territories, the fragmentation of religious authority led to greater tolerance and legal protections for Jews. However, these protections often didn't last, as borders frequently shifted and hostile Christian neighbors were an ever-present concern within Jewish communities in Europe.

The Polish-Lithuanian Commonwealth was one such place where some protections were afforded to Jews at points throughout history, only to be reneged or withdrawn. This area included large swaths of what came to be known as Galicia, which encompassed a large part of trans-Carpathia as well as parts of the Pale of the Settlement, an area where the Russian Empire would later restrict their Jews to living and doing business in. Though the population of Jews in these regions wouldn't grow substantially until the 19th century, Jews living in these parts of Eastern Europe during the Renaissance often came under attack by Kosack and Ruthenian neighbors.

Throughout Central Europe, in regions where Reformers held sway and adopted Luther's anti-Jewish positions, Jews faced renewed persecution. Expulsions, forced conversions, and restrictions on economic activities were common in parts of Europe still held by the Holy Roman Empire, as well as territories claimed by Protestants. In the Rhineland cities of Worms, Trier, and Metz, places where Jews had previously thrived, new clashes arose between Christians, leading to segregated places of worship for the two denominations, and a ban on marriage between Catholics and Protestants. This dynamic often saw Jews as an easy target from both sides of the theological chasm.

In parts of Northern and Eastern Europe where Protestantism gained a foothold, Jews were often pushed out. The populations sought refuge in even further-flung regions of Eastern Europe like trans-Carpathia or the burgeoning Ottoman Empire, where Sultan Bayezid II was more welcoming toward them, recognizing their potential to contribute to the Empire's economic and intellectual vitality. In Central Europe, despite the continued persecution of the Jews, big cultural changes were brewing.

The Enlightenment

Initially emerging in the late 17th century, the Enlightenment was characterized by its emphasis on secular and rational thought among intellectuals, writers, and scientists, eventually evolving into a widespread movement for reform.

Early on, proponents of Enlightenment values sought to modernize and liberalize fields such as theology, religious practices, education, and legal systems, aiming for a society more grounded in reason, openness, and scientific advancement, rather than traditionalist views.

As the movement progressed, it took on a political dimension, challenging the foundations of royal absolutism in favor of governmental structures that prioritized collective welfare over hereditary prestige and religious homogeneity. Thus, the period spanning from the late 17th century up through the 18th century became a pivotal era in European thought, marked by a newfound, widespread public appreciation for philosophy, reason, individualism, and secularism.

This period of reform in the political structures of Europe (and the secular culture at large) exerted a profound influence on Jewish communities. It catalyzed a movement toward emancipation from the restrictive conditions and ghettoization of the Renaissance and the persecution of the Reformation period. The Enlightenment also marked the beginning of a period of a marked transformation in Jewish thought, which would come to be known as the *Haskalah,* or Jewish Enlightenment, something we'll be focusing on in more detail in the next chapter.

For Jewish populations during this time, Enlightenment values served to catalyze the long-term struggle for a lasting Jewish emancipation from the chains of ages past. Enlightenment thinkers' emphasis on freedom, equality, and civil rights set the mechanisms in place for Jewish communities to start actively challenging the restrictive laws and social practices that had marginalized them for centuries in Europe, and for millennia across the full geographic footprint of their diasporic migratory paths. In Europe, especially during this time, Jews began to demand the civil rights they had so long been denied and also demanded an end to the restrictions that limited their participation in the emergent secular society.

Jewish thinkers of this era, such as Moses Mendelssohn, became instrumental in advocating for Jewish civil liberties in Europe; in Mendelssohn's case, within Prussia. His extensive body of work, encompassing writings and translations, helped bridge Jewish and European intellectual traditions while pushing the cause of Jewish emancipation across the continent. Mendelssohn's efforts helped make Jewish philosophical and religious thought accessible to wider audiences, which in turn, helped spread a greater understanding and appreciation of Jewish culture among non-Jewish Europeans.

Jewish Emancipation in Post-Enlightenment Europe

Alliances in politics and influential public spheres continued to be sought out by Jews in Europe during the time directly following the Enlightenment. The Jews of France found hope in the Revolution, and Napoleon himself aided the Jewish quest for emancipation through his policies during the Napoleonic Wars. By promoting principles of equality and integration for Jews in the territories under his control, Napoleon effectively challenged the entrenched social order and ignited widespread discussions on the rights of Jews. His actions paved the way for legislative and societal changes that advanced the cause of Jewish emancipation in various parts of Europe.

In Germany, figures such as Gabriel Riesser, a leading Jewish lawyer, worked tirelessly toward the struggle for Jewish equality. Through relentless advocacy and activism, Riesser became a central figure in the revolutionary movements of 1848. These aimed to implement liberal reforms across Europe, including the emancipation of Jews. His contributions were instrumental in advancing the legal and social status of Jewish people in Germany and beyond.

Jewish children born during the post-Enlightenment era emerged into a new world, one that held great promises for European Jews. Sigmund Freud, for instance, who was born in 1856 in Vienna, was one of the most influential Jewish thinkers born in this post-Enlightenment time. While firmly anchored in the concerns of the 19th and 20th centuries, his contributions were deeply rooted in the intellectual tradition that the Enlightenment promoted, blending science with humanistic inquiry to explore the depths of the human psyche.

Rise of Hasidism and Jewish Mysticism

While the Enlightenment set the wheels in motion for Jewish secular contributions to the arts, sciences, and culture in Europe well into the 19th century and beyond, it also allowed new branches of Jewish religious practice and dogmas to emerge. As the emergence of new political orders and more open, secular forms of Judaism were cast in the spotlight of the greater Enlightenment principles reshaping Europe, the rise of Hasidism and Jewish mysticism offered observant Jews a promise of spiritual renewal.

Hasidism

A new type of faith was called for against the backdrop of 18th-century Eastern Europe's social and religious turmoil, which still saw Catholics and Protestants clashing, with Jews as a convenient, mutual target. First originating from within the Polish-Lithuanian Commonwealth, Hasidism emerged as a response to the deepening crises affecting Eastern European Jewish communities, which were plagued by constant external threats and internal fragmentation.

Hasidism, which means "piety" or "loving-kindness" in Hebrew, was founded by a rabbi named Israel ben Eliezer in the early 18th century. In his teachings, ben Eliezer, who also came to be known as the *Baal Shem Tov,* or "Master of the Good Name," emphasized direct, personal communion with the divine, a joyful embrace of life, and a focus on the spiritual essence of religious practice, rather than solely on scholarly study. This represented a radical shift from the more austere, intellectual forms of Judaism that dominated at the time.

Central to Hasidic teaching is the concept of *devekut,* or clinging to God, which suggests that a continuous, passionate devotion can connect one to God even during mundane activities. ben Eliezer taught that prayer and simple faith could be more valuable than intellectual religious study, making spirituality accessible to people without formal education. Hasidism also introduced the idea of the *Tzaddik,* a righteous person who could serve as a spiritual leader and intermediary, guiding followers in their spiritual practice and connecting them directly to God.

Hasidism quickly spread across Eastern Europe, appealing to many Jews with its message of spiritual rejuvenation, communal worship, and the sanctification of daily life. It helped promote a sense of community and belonging, offering hope and a renewed sense of purpose to Jews who felt alienated by the challenges of the time. For the Jews of Central and Eastern Europe especially, this often included frequent persecution at the hands of their Christian neighbors, and grinding rural poverty.

The Hasidic movement led to the development of distinct Hasidic sects, each with its own practices but united by the core principles of joy, piety, and a direct, personal connection to God. Hasidism's cultural impact today has extended far beyond its spiritual teachings, influencing Jewish music, dance, and storytelling traditions and even some traditions practiced by other, less-observant denominations of Jews.

Despite initial opposition from more traditional Jewish leaders who viewed Hasidism's emphasis on mysticism and the central role of the *Tzaddik* with suspicion, the movement's energy, momentum, and promise to imbue everyday life with spiritual significance allowed it to significantly inform many aspects of Modern Jewish thought and practice.

Hasidism Today

The Hasidic movement's choice to maintain the same manner of dress as in the "old country," even after migrating to different parts of the world, is deeply rooted in spiritual and cultural reasons. This adherence to traditional attire, including the donning of *payot* and *tzitzit* for men, and the use of head coverings and wigs by women. To this day, they serve as a physical manifestation of the community's values, beliefs, and history, emphasizing continuity, identity, and resistance to assimilation.

Hasids normally stick to demure, black garb. For men, a central piece of their wardrobe is the *bekishe* or *rekel*, a long, black coat worn during the Sabbath and on weekdays, respectively. On their heads, adult men often wear a *shtreimel* or *spodik*, types of fur hats reserved for special occasions like the Sabbath and holidays. Daily garments include *tzitzit*, fringed garments worn beneath their shirts, and *tefillin,* holy scrolls bound with leather straps during weekday morning prayers. *Payot*, the uncut sidelocks, are grown in observance of a biblical commandment, complementing the traditional *kippah* or *yarmulke* worn on the head. During prayers, a *tallis*, or prayer shawl, is draped over their shoulders, completing their religious ensemble.

Hasidic women's attire is centered around the principles of modesty, or *Tzniut*, which dictates that clothes should cover the body adequately and not draw undue attention. Dresses or skirts are long, extending well below the knees, and tops are designed to cover the elbows and collarbone. After marriage, women cover their hair with a scarf, wig, or sometimes a hat, following the tradition that a woman's hair is reserved for her husband's eyes only. To further ensure modesty, opaque tights or leggings are worn under skirts. The specifics of these dress codes vary among different Hasidic communities, but the underlying principles of modesty and adherence to Jewish law are universally observed.

Jewish Mysticism

Jewish Mysticism, particularly through the Kabbalistic tradition, underwent a marked resurgence and transformation during the 18th century, continuing well into the post-Enlightenment era. This period was marked by a profound spiritual awakening across Jewish and non-Jewish populations that sought to reconcile the inner world of faith with the external changes brought about by the Enlightenment and modernity.

In the 18th century, the rise of the Baal Shem Tov and his Hasidic practices brought new life to ancient Kabbalistic mysticism. Although through today's lens it's easy to view Hassidism as a conservative, even fundamentalist movement, it's important to note that during the time it came into being, it served as a bridge that made mystical concepts accessible to the masses (albeit men only). This moved Kabbalah from the elite study circles of scholars to the heart of Jewish communal life. It was because of this accessibility that the teachings of the Baal Shem Tov and his successors spread rapidly through Eastern Europe. This created a spiritual revival that, in some ways, directly countered the rationalist tendencies of the *Haskalah*, or Jewish Enlightenment, a parallel movement that we'll focus on in greater detail in the coming chapter.

Hasidic leaders used mystical teachings to inspire their followers, emphasizing the importance of intention, or *kavanah*, and devotion, *devekut,* in making prayers and following divine *mitzvot,* commandments. This approach offered a spiritual path that was deeply personal and emotionally engaging, appealing to Jews across the social spectrum.

Into the 19th and 20th centuries, as the Jewish Enlightenment sought to integrate Jewish life into the broader cultural and intellectual currents of Europe, Jewish mysticism provided a necessary counterbalance. It helped preserve a distinct Jewish identity through its emphasis on the mystical and transcendent aspects of Judaism.

Figures such as Rabbi Nachman of Breslov, who was the great-grandson of Hasidism's founder, the Baal Shem Tov ben Eliezer, continued to innovate within this tradition, blending Kabbalistic mysticism with Hasidic joy and emphasizing personal spiritual struggle and the power of storytelling.

In the post-Enlightenment era, Kabbalah and Jewish mysticism faced new challenges and opportunities. The spread of secularism and the scientific worldview presented hurdles to mystical beliefs, yet the mystical tradition also found new audiences.

Still, the search for spiritual meaning in a rapidly changing world led many, including secular Jews and non-Jews, to explore Kabbalistic teachings. Kabbalah's universalist aspects, with its deep philosophical insights into the nature of the Divine and the universe, garnered interest from a broad spectrum of spiritual truth-seekers. This trend stretched well into the late 20th century, when, interestingly, Jewish mysticism was adopted by non-

Jewish celebrity pop-cultural presences, most notably Madonna.

Before We Move On

As we turn the page from the Enlightenment and its transformative effects on Jewish thought and society into the post-Enlightenment era, we can easily spot a distinct juxtaposition of emerging Jewish Enlightenment principles against the backdrop of a resurgence in devout worship and Jewish mysticism.

The Modern era for Jews was one of nuanced interactions between the simultaneous pursuit of rational enlightenment and a deepening of mystical spiritual practices. This showcased the Jewish community's dynamic adaptability and unyielding quest for meaning and identity.

The remainder of this book focuses specifically on modern Jewish movements and the ever-present struggle for true emancipation. We'll chart the course through the Jewish Enlightenment, the emergence of modern Zionism, and the impacts of World War II and the Holocaust on Jewish consciousness, all the way up to the establishment of the State of Israel and beyond.

The Modern era, characterized by upheaval and remarkable resilience, offers us an even more up-close view of how Jewish communities have successfully navigated the complexities of modernity, fought for their rights and recognition, and continued to innovate religiously, culturally, and politically, even in the face of pogroms, genocide, and lingering anti-Semitic threats that carry on until this day.

Chapter 8: Modern Movements and Emancipation

Enlightenment is man's emergence from his self-imposed immaturity. –Immanuel Kant

In a post-Enlightenment world awakening to groundbreaking modern ideas, the Jewish Enlightenment (or *Haskalah*) and the emergence of modern Jewish denominations represented a fundamental shift in Jewish thought and societal participation. In this chapter, we'll follow the journey of Jewish communities as they navigated the complex currents of these transformative times, again showcasing adaptation, struggle, and a spiritual and intellectual awakening that reshaped their collective identity and contributions to a rapidly evolving world. Jewish communities entering the modern age found themselves at the crossroads of historical upheaval and cultural blossoming.

But the sweeping changes that brought the world to post-Enlightenment times weren't insular. Amid the whirlwind of societal reformation and intellectual revival, Jewish communities engaged heavily with the broader cultural movements of their time, making active contributions to the arts, sciences, and commerce while grappling with the quest for recognition and rights. It was during this time that the emergence of Hasidism and Jewish mysticism aimed to crack away at some of the spiritual and existential queries that Jews came to confront in this new enlightened world. However, this movement, though aimed at the masses, was not for everyone, and a new strain of secular Judaism was born.

Through the lens of the *Haskalah* movement and the rise of modern Jewish denominations, we can trace the evolution of Jewish life and thought, revealing how these developments influenced Jewish identity and laid the groundwork for future contributions to the arts, sciences, and culture worldwide.

The Haskalah Movement

The Haskalah movement first emerged in Europe in the late 18th century, embodying a profound shift in Jewish intellectual life. Inspired by the broader European Enlightenment, rather than the mysticism of Hasidism, the Haskalah movement championed reason, intellectual freedom, and secular knowledge, while emphasizing the maintenance of a distinct Jewish identity. It advocated for the integration of Jews into European society through education reform, encouraging the study of secular subjects alongside traditional religious texts, the adoption of European dress and manners, and loyalty to the ruling powers of the time.

Influenced by the prevailing secular Enlightenment principles of this era, Jewish thinkers began to advocate for a new form of Judaism that engaged with the world around it on a deeper level, both intellectually and culturally. This era saw the emergence of prominent Jewish philosophers, including Moses Mendelssohn. Mendelssohn advocated for a balance between Jewish tradition and engagement with European culture and philosophy.

The movement's proponents, known as *maskilim*, sought to combine traditional Jewish values with contemporary European culture, promoting a series of reforms in Jewish education, religious practice, and community life. This intellectual awakening paved the way for several key transformations within Jewish communities and set the precedent for the splitting-off of various factions, which would eventually become modern Jewish denominations such as Orthodox, Reform, and Conservative Judaism.

Modern Jewish Denominations

Orthodox Judaism is rooted in a steadfast adherence to traditional Jewish law, or *Halacha*, and Jewish customs, or *Minhag*. It first emerged as a response to the challenges posed by modernity and the Haskalah movement. Emphasizing the immutable nature of the *Torah* and the commandments, Orthodox Judaism seeks to maintain continuity with the past while maintaining a continuous engagement with the present. It's characterized by a broad range of practices and beliefs, from the ultra-Orthodox, who strictly observe

Jewish law, to the Modern Orthodox, who choose to integrate more into secular society while still upholding general *Halachic* principles.

Reform Judaism originated in the early 19th century as a radical departure from traditional Orthodoxy, embodying the spirit of the Haskalah's call for change. It emphasized individual autonomy in interpreting Jewish traditions and texts, advocating for a Judaism that evolves in response to contemporary ethical and social challenges. Reform Judaism has advocated for more progressive policies within the Jewish community, including a greater emphasis on gender equality.

Conservative Judaism, developed in the late 19th century, seeks a middle ground between the strict observance of Orthodox Judaism and the more secular-informed approaches of Reform Judaism. It upholds the authority of Jewish law but allows for adaptation and change guided by contemporary scholarship and democratic decision-making within the Jewish community. Conservative Judaism strives to preserve Jewish tradition while recognizing the need for evolution in practice and belief.

The Haskalah movement's legacy is seen in the diversity of modern Jewish denominations, each reflecting different interpretations of Jewish identity, tradition, and engagement with the world. Through their distinct approaches to Jewish law, ritual, and ethical living, these denominations continue to shape contemporary Jewish life, highlighting the enduring influence of Enlightenment ideals on Jewish thought and community.

Contributions to Arts, Sciences, and Politics

When we look at the contributions that modern Jews have made to the arts, sciences, and politics, it becomes clear how the Haskalah movement's embrace of Enlightenment ideals paved the way for achievements that stretched far beyond the confines of religious and community life and the distinct denominations of Judaism.

This transition into broader societal engagement, spurred by the Haskalah movement, marked an important expansion of the Jewish spirit of inquiry and contribution. It reflected an evolution from internal community reform to a series of greater impacts on the global stage. Since then, Jewish thinkers, artists, and activists, inspired by the ideals of reason, freedom, and equality, have ventured into new territories of expression and innovation.

This cultural transition from the core of Jewish Enlightenment into the wider world showcases the dynamic interplay between Jewish identity and universal human progress. It illustrates how Jewish engagement with contemporary thought and society has not only enriched Jewish religious life and cultural customs but also made lasting contributions to our collective cultural, scientific, and political heritage.

The Arts

In the arts, modern Jews have played an important role. As we explored in the previous chapter, the tradition of Jewish artists and artisans in Europe can be traced back to the Italian Renaissance, when Jewish scholars and artists thrived. The work of Jewish artists in Europe, whether in the visual arts, music, or literature, often carried subtle references to Jewish heritage and identity, serving as a bridge between their Jewish roots and the wider cultural milieu they inhabited. By the 20th century, following waves of immigration, especially to America, the contributions of Jewish artists became even more pronounced across various domains of art. However, many Jewish artists were still living in Europe at this time despite widespread persecution.

For example, Marc Chagall, the Belarusian-French Jewish painter, with his fantastical scenes imbued with Jewish life and folklore, brought a unique perspective to modern art, blending his Jewish heritage with avant-garde European artistic movements. Writers like Prague-born Franz Kafka, through his bracing literary works, explored the existential complexities of modern existence, reflecting the alienation and existential quests that paralleled the Jewish experience in Europe. Though the Spanish Inquisition left a dearth of Sephardic Jewish artists on the Iberian peninsula, some, including modern artists such as Joan Miró, created works of art that transcended specific cultural narratives and engaged with universal themes of freedom and creativity.

In music, Jewish-American composers and performers like Irving Berlin and Leonard Bernstein made indelible marks on American music and Broadway, infusing their compositions with the nuances of their cultural identity. On the avant-garde side of music composition, serialist composer Arnold Schoenberg, who was born Jewish but converted to Protestantism in his early 20s, pioneered twelve-tone music. Though Schoenberg chose to seek meaning outside the faith he was born into, his decision and his pioneering work reflect the broader quest for identity and meaning among Jews in modern times.

The entertainment landscape in America was heavily shaped by Jewish talent, particularly through the emergence of the Borscht Belt. This Jewish resort area in the Catskill Mountains became a hotbed for comedic talent, nurturing the careers of many Jewish comedians who would go on to define American humor.

The modern era also saw the rise of Jewish celebrities in film and television, like Hungarian-Jewish actress and socialite Zsa Zsa Gabor and vaudevillians George Burns and Jack Benny. Both were born in America to Jewish immigrants and brought their unique personalities and backgrounds to the screen, enriching American popular culture.

The foundational role of Jewish moguls in building Hollywood's film industry in the early part of the 20th century can't be overstated. Figures like

Louis B. Mayer and Marcus Loew, who started MGM Pictures were instrumental in establishing the American film industry. Their efforts not only transformed the entertainment landscape but also provided a platform for Jewish artists and stories, contributing to a broader understanding and appreciation of Jewish culture and experiences.

The Sciences

Jewish contributions to the sciences and medicine during the 19th and 20th centuries represent a remarkable chapter in the history of human knowledge. In this period, Jewish thinkers, often facing considerable challenges, made groundbreaking advancements that have had a lasting impact on humanity.

The German-Jewish genius and Nobel prize-winner Albert Einstein was perhaps the most famous physicist of the 20th century and one of the most famous scientists of all time. He revolutionized our understanding of the universe with his theories of relativity, fundamentally altering the fields of physics and cosmology. His Jewish identity, coupled with his unparalleled discoveries in astrophysics, made him a symbol of perseverance and intellectual brilliance.

In medicine, another Nobel prize-winning German Jew was Paul Ehrlich. His medical research laid the foundation for modern immunology and chemotherapy. His discovery of the first effective treatment for syphilis represented a monumental step forward in medical science, showcasing the potential for targeted therapeutic strategies.

Rosalind Franklin, a British-Jewish woman conducted pioneering research on the molecular structures of DNA. Though underrecognized during her lifetime, her discoveries have been useful in the development of modern genetics. Her pioneering X-ray image technique allowed scientists to identify the unique double helix structure of DNA for the first time, something we take for granted today.

Sigmund Freud, an Austrian Jew, was the father of psychoanalysis. He opened new pathways in understanding the human mind and behavior. His theories on the unconscious mind have profoundly influenced modern psychology, literature, and the arts, bringing to light the complexity of human nature.

In the field of biochemistry, the Russian-born Chaim Weizmann developed pioneering industrial fermentation processes and later moved into politics, playing a role in the Zionist movement, which eventually led to Israel's establishment. He straddled the world of science and politics and went on to serve as the President of Israel.

Politics

Throughout the 19th and 20th centuries, Jewish figures played an important part in shaping political landscapes across Europe, America, and Israel.

In the United Kingdom, Benjamin Disraeli became a prominent figure in the 19th century and was notable for being the first (and thus far only) Jewish-born person to serve as Prime Minister. Even though he grew up Baptist after his father had a falling out with his local synagogue, Disraeli still held on to his Jewish roots through his surname which went unchanged.

In continental Europe, journalist and activist Theodor Herzl gave birth to political Zionism in Austria-Hungary and laid the groundwork for the eventual establishment of an Israeli state in Palestine. His vision and leadership rallied Jewish communities and sympathetic supporters around the world toward the goal of a Jewish homeland in the Holy Land, a subject that we'll be covering in more detail in the next chapter.

Over in France, Leon Blum stood out for his progressive policies and eventually served as the first Jewish Prime Minister of France, where he implemented a series of social reforms in the 1930s. Decades later, Simone Veil, a Holocaust survivor whose family had been in Auschwitz, advanced women's rights through her work as a magistrate and health minister. Her work was instrumental in the decriminalization of abortion in the 1970s.

The U.S. has seen several Jewish political figures contribute to the nation's fabric. Louis Brandeis and Felix Frankfurter, both Supreme Court Justices in the early to mid-20th century, were instrumental in shaping American legal thought and civil rights.

Though often maligned for his role in the Vietnam War, Henry Kissinger, a German Jew, served as Secretary of State under Presidents Nixon and Ford, playing a key role in U.S. foreign policy, diplomacy, and war. Working in opposition to Kissinger's hawkish approach, countless Jewish-American activists, including the Brooklyn-born Bernard Sanders, became involved in groups like the Student Nonviolent Coordinating Committee (SNCC).

Sanders later went on to become a prominent U.S. representative, senator, and eventual Democratic presidential candidate. In the 1970s, before Sanders launched his political career, Bella Abzug, a Jewish politician known for her work on women's rights, gay rights, and environmentalism, stood as a powerful, progressive Jewish-American voice in Congress.

Once the State of Israel had been established, Golda Meir, one of the founding members of Israel and its fourth prime minister, showed strong leadership during some of its most challenging times, including the Yom Kippur War. Born in Kyiv and having emigrated to the United States before settling in what would become Israel, Meir's political career was marked by her relentless dedication to the Israeli people and the Zionist cause. As prime minister, she focused on strengthening the country amidst regional tensions, never wavering in her commitment to her nation's security and prosperity.

Jewish Life in the Americas and New Communities

The narrative of Jewish immigration to the Americas, particularly from 1820 through 1924, stands as an important chapter in Jewish history. It's a story of aspiration, adversity, and the same remarkable fortitude that had characterized Jewish people up to the modern era.

The modern age marked a period of changes for those in the Diaspora, particularly in Eastern Europe, as they sought refuge from economic hardship, persecution at the hands of their Christian neighbors, and the fundamental shifts brought on by the 19th century, which included industrialization and urbanization. Immigrants who left for the new world were drawn to the promise of the "Golden Land" of America and the promise of a better future, and in many cases, they found it.

Initially, the influx of Jewish immigrants came to the U.S. predominantly from Central Europe. They didn't confine themselves to the rapidly-growing urban centers of the East Coast, but rather, started to spread across the United States, establishing roots in cities across the Midwest, some even making it as far as California. This period witnessed an exponential growth in the Jewish population in America, ballooning 100-fold from only 3,000 in 1820 to around 300,000 by 1880 (*A Century of*

Immigration, 1820-1924 - from Haven to Home: 350 Years of Jewish Life in America, 2019).

In Canada, Jewish immigration began slowly but steadily throughout the 19th century, with a wave of growth coinciding with the U.S. Jewish immigration wave in the early 20th century. Jewish communities in Canada established themselves in major cities such as Montreal, Toronto, and Vancouver, where they played a part in developing Canada's cultural, economic, and social fabric. Today, Canada remains a top destination for francophone Jewish immigrants.

The post-World War II era saw a major influx of Jewish immigrants to North America, including many Holocaust survivors, which led to further population growth. Canada currently boasts the fourth-largest Jewish population in the world, while the U.S. holds the largest population of Jews in the world—even greater than in Israel itself, according to Jewish Virtual Library's 2023 Statistics (*Jewish Population of the World*, 2023).

In their new homelands, Jewish communities in North America faced the dual challenge of preserving their rich cultural and religious heritage while assimilating into broader society. They encountered and combated anti-Semitism, forging pathways to economic success and social acceptance through resilience and adaptability. The establishment of synagogues, schools, and community organizations played a critical role in maintaining Jewish traditions and fostering a sense of unity and support among these burgeoning communities.

But the U.S. and Canada weren't the only places Jewish immigrants went during this transformative era. As Europe faced economic hardship, persecution, and the dramatic upheavals of the 19th and early 20th centuries, Latin America was also a destination for those seeking new beginnings. There, as in the U.S., Jewish immigrants had a chance to start anew.

Many Sephardic Jews from the Ottoman Empire and Ashkenazi Jews from Eastern Europe found their way down to Mexico, integrating into Mexican society while maintaining their cultural and religious identity. Over time, Mexico's Jewish population has contributed to various aspects of Mexican culture and economy, maintaining a distinct presence within the country's diverse social landscape

In the wake of newly-found independence from colonial rule, many Central and South American countries also saw an influx of Jewish immigrants. Initially, small numbers of Sephardic Jewish settlers from Morocco made their way to the northeastern coast of Brazil, later expanding into the Amazon region, while others from the Caribbean islands settled in Venezuela, Colombia, Panama, and Costa Rica. This period also saw arrivals to these countries from Central Europe, Germany, France, and England.

The major wave of organized Jewish immigration to Latin America began following the May Laws of

1881 in the Russian Empire, which severely impacted the Jews in the Pale of Settlement. Argentina and Brazil became top destinations, with the Jewish population in Argentina increasing by the early 20th century with the influx of Ashkenazi Jews from Central and Eastern Europe.

By 1930, Argentina had become home to a large part of Latin America's Jewish population, thanks to its liberal immigration policy and the establishment of agricultural settlements by the Jewish Colonization Association (JCA). Ironically, the country would later become a popular relocation for German Nazi officers looking to shirk culpability for the Holocaust, and the Argentine government even sponsored a program that allowed large numbers of Nazis to seek refuge there (Klein, 2018).

Even smaller countries like Bolivia saw Jewish communities flourish, especially after the first large wave of Jewish immigration during the 1930s. By the end of World War II, Bolivia had a considerable Jewish population, though many would continue their journey to other countries in search of better opportunities.

Brazil, with its large geographic footprint, attracted Jewish immigrants throughout the 19th and early 20th centuries. Brazil's Jewish community continued to grow, contributing to the country's development and cultural diversity. Today, Brazil hosts the 10th largest Jewish community in the world (*Brazil Virtual Jewish History Tour*, n.d.).

In Chile, where Jews also settled, Jewish immigrants achieved prominence in various fields, from arts and culture to politics and commerce, again highlighting the integral role they have played in shaping the societies of their adopted countries all over the Americas.

Before We Move On

With a deeper understanding of how Jewish people defined themselves in the modern era, and where around the world they went, we now turn to the defining movement in modern Jewish history— the rise of Zionism and the quest for statehood. As emigrants fled Europe, others sought to carve out a new home in Palestine.

The next chapter will guide us through the birth of Zionism to the creation of the State of Israel. From Herzl's initial visions of a Jewish state to the tumultuous events leading up to the declaration of Israeli independence in 1948, we'll examine the political, social, and cultural underpinnings that fueled the Zionist movement and some of the controversy this ethnic-nationalist political theory has brought with it.

Chapter 9: Zionism and Statehood

What compels a nation to emerge from the shadows of the Diaspora? What drives disparate groups to unite under the banner of ancient dreams in the land of their common forefathers? This chapter is all about the Judeo-centric political theory that is Zionism. It is a movement based on the enduring yearning for a Jewish homeland—the desire for a sanctuary where a people dispersed (and everywhere a minority) can live in peace, free from the persecution that has historically plagued them.

Zionism's story is one of aspiration and struggle, one that needs to be framed against the backdrop of global shifts, the waning Ottoman Empire, and the complex dynamics of Jewish life in Central and

Eastern Europe at the time of the movement's founding. Its narrative is punctuated by the *Aliyot*, the waves of immigration that saw hordes of Jewish immigrants make their way to a foreign land. Though many of these migrants knew nothing of the Middle East, at the same time, *Eretz Yisra'el*, or Palestine as it was called at the time, was a place they all knew well through millennia of *Torah* study.

The Development and Ideologies of Zionism

The rise of Zionism as a powerful movement in the late 19th and early 20th centuries marked a rather drastic turning point in Jewish history. Its roots can be traced back to the ancient Jewish connection to Palestine, or, *Eretz Yisra'el* (the Land of Israel), and the pressing need for a solution to the escalating crises facing Jewish communities in Eastern and Central Europe. The term "Zionism" derives from Zion itself, one of the hills of ancient Jerusalem, the likely eventual destination of proto-Judeo tribes when the Hyksos "Shepherd King" dynasty was expelled from the Nile basin up into the highlands. It was also the place they had returned to when liberated from Babylon by King Cyrus of Persia.

The ideological underpinnings of Zionism are heavily informed by the pervasive anti-Semitism Jews have faced for millennia in places around the world. It was also based on economic restrictions and a nationalistic fervor that began to sweep through

Europe, even well before Fascism and the Italian poet Gabriele D'Annunzio, who pioneered proto-Fascism, seized Fiume (today Rijeka, Croatia), declaring it an independent state in 1919.

While in some ways Zionism can be considered a reactionary movement against widespread anti-Semitism, it can't be considered an inherently anti-Fascist movement. An important thing to note here is that Zionism is largely rooted in personal, direct experience and trauma-informed realities. Any political or ideological sentiments that surround it are, in a way, secondary to this main driving factor—which, it should be said, given the history of the Jewish people, is legitimate.

The reality is that, for thousands of years, as we've seen in previous chapters, Jewish people faced intense persecution and were often scapegoated for societal problems. This often led to ghettoization, widespread pogroms in Europe, and discriminatory laws that severely restricted their rights and opportunities. This hostile environment was widespread throughout the Western world for millennia and also became prevalent in parts of the Near East once Israel's statehood was declared by Zionists in 1948.

These undeniable factors, coupled with the aggregate experiences of Jews in Europe, inspired thinkers and leaders of the community to seek a lasting solution to the so-called "Jewish Question." The "question" at hand was not a question but rather a series of questions that pertained to the status of

Jewish people in European countries and where they "belonged."

Zionism, in the mind of its drafters, was an opportunity for self-determination rather than just waiting around for the inevitable to happen once again, which it did. Once the Nazis seized power in Germany in 1933, it became especially clear that, in some regards, the Zionist idea was not simply a nationalistic ideology. The Nazi threat made Zionism seem like a highly practical act of foresight and preemptive self-defense against a clear tide of rising anti-Semitism.

Theodor Herzl was the father of modern political Zionism. By seizing on this moment and the real threats at hand, Herzl successfully transformed the yearning for a return to Zion from a passive hope to an active political movement with the ultimate goal of an Israeli state. In his seminal work *Der Judenstaat* (The Jewish State) of 1896, Herzl argued that a sovereign Jewish state was the only solution to the persecution of Jews worldwide.

One of Herzl's key assertions was that Jews would never be fully accepted as equals in their host countries. This ran somewhat contrary to what Jews had demonstrated over time and were very actively manifesting at the time he was writing *Der Judenstaat*. For thousands of years, adaptive strategies had been exhibited by Jews, including continual acclimation to new homes abroad, going all the way back to the Babylonian Captivity. This, paired with the drive toward continual modernization which had been in place at least since the Haskalah movement began in the late 18th century, meant that the Jews were well-poised to successfully integrate into Western European and American society as the 20th century approached. Herzl's ideas, however, noted that the patterns of persecution would likely thwart such efforts and that the types of adaptations and compromises that Jews had learned to live with over millennia were not effective strategies moving forward. Zionism said "enough" to being considered second-class, and "yes" to a new form of Jewish militancy that endures to this day. It most notably appears in the state of Israel itself, which was founded largely on Herzl's political theories put forward in *Der Judenstaat* as well as his fears and doubts, which many Jews embraced as their common touchstone.

Two of the key figures who rallied around Herzl's ideas were Max Nordau and Israel Zangwill, both of whom became highly influential in shaping Zionist thought. Nordau, a close ally of Herzl, brought his background as a physician and essayist to advocate for the cause. Zangwill, meanwhile, was instrumental in promoting the concept of a Jewish homeland, at times advocating for Jewish resettlement in territories outside of Palestine, including, oddly, Uganda and Galveston, Texas.

Though in Herzl the Zionist idea had a founder to some extent, Zionism as a political and cultural theory quickly evolved into a more diverse movement with various ideologies and visions for a future

Jewish state. These ranged from Herzl's political Zionism, which emphasized diplomatic and political efforts to secure a homeland, to cultural Zionism, advocated by figures like Ahad Ha'am (Asher Ginsberg), who stressed the revival of ancient Jewish culture and the Hebrew language as the foundation of a new Jewish national identity.

Both political and cultural Zionism had strong right-wing undercurrents, but there were also leftist movements such as Labor Zionism, another branch that was oriented toward socialist principles and the establishment of a society based on egalitarianism and communal labor. This lead to the eventual creation of the *kibbutz* system of agricultural communes throughout Palestine.

Other notable ideologies within the greater Zionist movement included religious Zionism and revisionist Zionism. Religious Zionism merged traditional Jewish religious beliefs with Zionist nationalism, advocating for the return to Zion as a fulfillment of biblical prophecy. Revisionist Zionism, founded by Ze'ev Jabotinsky, advocated for a more militant approach to establishing a Jewish state that would have an even wider footprint in the region.

There were some even more extreme movements. A few embraced principles of Fascism when that movement was still in its infancy. Radical Jewish artists living in Mandatory Palestine in the 1930s, for example, created Canaanism, an extreme right-wing movement and form of cultural Zionism. Canaanism was crafted in the image of early Italian

Fascism. It sought to go back even further than the existence of a distinct Jewish people and revert to the ancient practices and modes of the Canaanites.

There were also Zionist terrorist and paramilitary factions. These were active from the 1920s through the 1940s. Their main goal was to snuff out any opposition. The victims of their attacks were often local Arab civilians.

Despite the differences between all these distinct Zionist factions, and following the intellectual tradition of debating among Jews, these diverse streams of Zionism were successfully melded together. Under the banner of Zionism, a coalition somehow arose, one with the joint purpose of carving out a Jewish homeland in Palestine.

This goal was pursued through various means but mainly focused on the promotion of Jewish immigration (*Aliyah*) and the establishment of Jewish settlements. The movement's efforts led to the declaration of the State of Israel in 1948. This was a watershed moment for Zionists, but for the Arab populations already living in Palestine it would come to be known as the *Nakba*, or "catastrophe."

Zionist ideologies were varied, and the movement's key figures were sometimes at odds with each other. The common purpose that brought them together was the creation of a Jewish state in Palestine. This compromise would have implications for the Arab populations of the region and would fundamentally change what it meant to be Jewish for Diasporic Jews across the world.

Jewish Immigration to Palestine

The waves of Jewish immigration to Palestine that began at the tail end of the 19th century, known as *Aliyah*, played a major role in the development of modern Israel and its societal fabric. These migrations weren't just mass movements of people due to hardship and strife experienced in Europe, though for a significant amount of migrants, this was the case. Rather, these waves of mass migration were part of a strategic vision, one that was directly aligned with Zionist ideology. Each wave, while driven by similar underlying motivations, brought its subtle distinctions and unique set of particularities.

Pre-State Aliyot (Migrations)

The First Aliyah (1882–1903)

The First Aliyah was motivated by Zionist ideology, the escape from anti-Semitic violence, and economic hardship in Eastern Europe. During this immigration wave, up to 35,000 Jews moved to Palestine. At the time, the Levant was part of the Ottoman Empire (*Aliyah*, 2024). They were driven by the dream of returning to their ancestral homeland and establishing a new life with agricultural settlements, which with the next wave, would come to be known as *kibbutzim*. This period saw the foundation of the first modern Jewish settlements, including Rishon LeZion, Petah Tikva, and Zichron Yaakov, despite facing difficulties such as malaria, lack of resources, and Ottoman bureaucratic obstacles.

The Second Aliyah (1904–1914)

The Second Aliyah was sparked by the 1903 Kishinev pogrom, erupting in the Moldovan city of the same name, which at that time was part of the Russian Empire. This massacre of Jews, along with other anti-Semitic attacks throughout the Russian Empire, the Pale of Settlement, and Jewish Galicia, inspired thousands more to seek refuge in Palestine. Again, around 35,000 to 40,000 Jews immigrated during this wave, bringing with them socialist ideals that led to the establishment of the first *kibbutz*, Degania, and the formation of the Jewish labor union, the *Histadrut* (*Second Aliyah*, 2024). This wave of *olim* (immigrants) contributed to the Hebrew cultural revival and the construction of the city of Tel Aviv.

The Third Aliyah (1919–1923)

With the signing of the Treaty of Versailles in 1919, vast swaths of territories previously controlled by the Central Powers were now under occupation by the Allies. In the case of Palestine, which was held by the British in the aftermath of the war, a mandate system was put into place.

The stated purpose of this British mandate was simply to have the war's victors administer the newly emerging states until they could become independent. To this day some still see the system as a "thinly veiled form of colonialism and occupation" (Tahhan, 2018, para. 8).

To frame the terms of and justify the British Mandate once the Ottoman Empire finally toppled in 1922, the British relied on a wartime document that became the focal point of a much-contested two-sided promise the British made both to Zionists and Arab Palestinians. The Balfour Declaration, which was a letter written by United Kingdom Foreign Secretary Arthur Balfour to influential Jewish-British magnate Lord Rothschild during the war, promised support for a "national home for the Jewish people" in Palestine. Known as "Balfour's Promise" to Arab Palestinians, the document also guaranteed them certain protections.

The Declaration and the British mandate were seen by Zionists as an open invitation to settle in Palestine. This kicked off the Third Aliyah, which brought around 40,000 immigrants to Palestine (*Aliyah*, 2024). These new *olim* were driven by a growing Zionist fervor that was newly empowered by the Declaration and the Mandate, but also by a deep desire to start anew after the great war had ravaged Europe. The *olim* of the Third Aliyah contributed to the expansion of agricultural settlements in Palestine and the strengthening of Jewish self-defense organizations.

The Fourth Aliyah (1924–1929)

Economic hardship and anti-Semitic policies in Poland and Hungary prompted the Fourth Aliyah, with around 80,000 Jews arriving (*Aliyah*, 2024). Unlike earlier waves, many of these immigrants to Palestine were middle-class families who moved to urban areas, boosting the economy but also exacerbating tensions with Arab populations due to land and job competition.

The Fifth Aliyah (1929-1939)

The rise of Nazism and the subsequent Jewish persecution in Europe led to the Fifth Aliyah, with over 250,000 Jews fleeing Europe for Palestine (*Aliyah*, 2024). This wave of immigration was characterized by the growth of urban populations, the establishment of new industries, and significant cultural contributions from highly-educated Jews who were fleeing the Nazis. This Aliyah, however, also marked yet another escalation in Arab-Jewish tensions, which eventually led to the 1936–1939 Arab Revolt.

The Arab Revolt (1936-1939)

This period was marked by widespread protests, strikes, and violent clashes. The Revolt led to political and social repercussions, shaping the future landscape of the Middle East and laying the groundwork for further conflict between Jewish and Arab communities in Palestine.

The sudden influx of over 250,000 Jews into Palestine from Europe as World War II raged on was propelled by the urgent need to escape Nazism and persecution, but it ultimately threatened stability in the region. The Balfour Declaration, aside from acknowledging support for the Zionist cause, had promised Arab Palestinians that their civil and religious rights would be upheld.

While Britain made these bold promises to both sides through the Balfour Declaration, they also made some contradictory back-door promises to Arab leaders, hinting at independence for Arab lands under Ottoman control if they supported the Allies in World War I. This duality led to competing expectations and claims over Palestine, complicating the region's political landscape. A revolt broke out in fierce opposition to British colonial rule and the perceived neglect of the autonomy and rights Palestinian Arabs believed they'd been promised under the British Mandate.

The Path to a Jewish State (1939–1948)

Though the Revolt ceased in 1939, the path to Jewish independence from that point onward was still characterized by ongoing tensions and conflict with Arab Palestinian neighbors. This period saw the intensification of the Zionist movement and ongoing tensions between the three parties, as both Zionists and Arabs had issues with British control and the dual promises made.

The escalating tensions eventually culminated in the British withdrawal from Palestine in 1948, marking the end of the Mandate period and representing a pivotal moment for Zionists, who saw this power vacuum as the opportunity they were waiting for. In announcing its intention to leave Palestine, Britain essentially deferred the issue of Israeli statehood to the United Nations (UN). This decision led directly to the UN Partition Plan and subsequently to the declaration of the State of Israel, significantly altering the geopolitical landscape of the Middle East.

Following the UN's 1947 Partition Plan, which suggested dividing Palestine into independent Jewish and Arab states, tensions escalated further. The situation worsened with events like the Deir Yassin Massacre and the ambush of a Jewish convoy, exacerbating the conflict as the imminent British withdrawal approached. This period was characterized by an escalation in Jewish-Arab hostilities, setting the stage for further violence and retaliation.

The British officially ended their mandate in Palestine through the Palestine Bill of April 29, 1948, with a public statement from the Colonial and Foreign Office confirming the termination of British administration from midnight on May 14, 1948. This decision marked the conclusion of British governance in the region, setting the stage for the declaration of the State of Israel which took place that same day.

The declaration of Israeli statehood immediately triggered a reaction from Arab Palestinians who vehemently contested the claim of the Zionists, whom they saw as foreign occupiers. War broke out, and the *Nakba,* or "catastrophe" in Arabic, began. To

Zionists, who emerged as the victors, it was simply called the War of Independence, and it came to be a defining moment of national pride and glory.

During the war, Israel's statehood was cemented, and around 430,000 Palestinians were displaced, leading to a profound and lasting impact on the region and putting into motion the ongoing conflict between the State of Israel and the Palestinian people. During the time that stretched between 1947 and 1949 alone, at least a quarter of a million Palestinians in total were pushed out, most becoming refugees (*The Nakba Did Not Start or End in 1948*, 2017).

Post-Statehood Aliyot

Arab-Jewish Refugees (1948–1968)

With the outbreak of the war in 1948, Arab Jews who were living in countries throughout the Middle East and North Africa including Iraq, Yemen, Libya, Morocco, Algeria, Tunisia, Egypt, and Iran, began to migrate to Israel. These *olim* were driven by persecution risks and a growing active opposition to the Zionist vision across the pan-Arab world in the wake of the *Nakba*.

The Six-Day War in 1968 marked another threat to Jewish communities dispersed throughout the Arab world, exacerbating the pressures they already faced. This conflict led to renewed waves of migration as fears of retaliation and increased hostility from their Arab neighbors compelled many to seek safety in Israel. The aftermath of the Six-Day War saw an acceleration in the exodus of Jews from countries such as Egypt and Iraq, where communities had previously persisted despite growing tensions.

After Israel's swift victory in the Six-Day War, anti-Zionist and anti-Semitic sentiments across the Arab world continued to drive this migration well into the early 1970s, often requiring Jews to leave behind properties and possessions. Presently, very few Jewish communities exist in the Middle East outside Israel, having significantly dwindled in size during this time.

Ethiopian-Jewish Migration (late 1970s–early 1990s)

Ethiopian Jews, or *Beta Israel*, started migrating to Israel in small numbers around 1934, but mass immigration didn't begin until the late 1970s to early 1980s. In the lead-up to Operation Moses, which took place in 1984, thousands of Ethiopian Jews fled to Sudan, facing perilous journeys with around 4,000 losing their lives (Lipman, 2019). Despite initial secrecy, external pressures halted the airlifts, stranding many of the migrants trying to make their way to Israel.

Operation Solomon was the second mass migration of Ethiopian Jews, which took place in 1991 amid Ethiopia's escalating civil war. Over 14,000 Ethiopians were evacuated to Israel in 36 hours, demonstrating Israel's impressive commitment to their pledge to continue bringing in

Jewish communities under threat (*Operation Solomon*, n.d.).

Post-Soviet Jewish Migration (late 1980s–early 2000s)

The rapid decline and fall of the Soviet Union saw about 1.6 million Soviet Jews and their families immigrate to Israel (*1990s Post-Soviet Aliyah*, 2024). This mass migration was facilitated by the opening of Eastern borders under Mikhail Gorbachev. The wave of migrants from former Soviet countries had substantial implications for Israel's "Law of Return," as a large percentage of these secularized Soviet-Jewish immigrants were not considered Jewish under Orthodox interpretations. They were, however, eligible for Israeli citizenship. This wave included a diverse group of Ashkenazi and Mizrahi Jews hailing from all across the vast territory of the former Soviet Union, who once again altered Israel's demographic and cultural landscape.

Zionist Multiculturalism

The distinct and diverse waves of Jewish immigration to Palestine have fostered a modern pluralistic society in today's State of Israel, albeit one still deeply rooted in Zionist ideology. This amalgamation of cultures, traditions, and histories from diverse Jewish Diasporas has enriched Israel's societal fabric, creating a unique national identity that is both culturally varied and firmly anchored in Herzl's vision for a Jewish state.

Before We Move On

As we conclude the chapter on Zionism and the emergence of a nation, we pivot to one of the most harrowing epochs in Jewish history: the Holocaust. In this devastating, brutal genocide, we see the profound impact it has come to exert on modern Jewish identity and the indelible mark it made on the Jewish people.

Trigger Warning

The following chapter contains themes of genocide, death, and violence through descriptions of the historical events of the Holocaust. Reader discretion is advised for those who may find such content distressing or triggering.

Chapter 10: The Holocaust

For the dead and the living, we must bear witness. –Elie Wiesel

We face a stark reminder through the tragedy of the Holocaust, the Nazi Genocide which left six million European Jews dead. But the victims of the Nazi's brutal campaign went even further than the mass execution of Jews, as other ethnic minorities, such as Romani, disabled people, and homosexuals were also targeted.

As we navigate the shadows cast by one of history's darkest hours, it's important to remember and reflect. In the devastating brutality endured by millions of European Jews, we must also recognize the extraordinary strength of spirit that emerged in the most dire of circumstances. Jews, finding themselves in the darkest of places, kept their traditions alive; non-Jewish collaborators in countries such as France, Holland, and Italy stowed Jews away and mounted resistance campaigns against Nazi occupiers. The devastation of the Holocaust and the memories still held by any survivors today attest to the perseverance and strength of the Jews.

The Rise of Anti-Semitism and the Nazism

The hatred and targeting of Jews has a long, unfortunate history in Europe, rooted deeply in the soil of the continent's past and its religious history. As we reviewed in Chapter 6, medieval Europe's religious and social landscapes were characterized by an enduring prejudice against Jewish people, often stemming from economic envy due to Christian usury laws that made Jews the de-factor lenders, as well as general religious intolerance.

As we looked at previously through clear examples such as pogroms against the Jews as far back as the late 12th century, the ghettoization of Jews in Venice in 1516, the hostility against the Jews of Europe seen during the Middle Ages continued into the Renaissance and became institutionalized through edicts that restricted their rights. This led to their further marginalization. The periodic outbursts of violence against them continued well into the late

17th and 18th centuries when Enlightenment values swept with a glimmer of hope for the possibility that the ever-present scapegoating could end.

While some Enlightenment thinkers advocated for religious tolerance and Jewish emancipation, in line with the era's emphasis on liberty and equality, these progressive views were not universally adopted. Throughout 18th-century Europe, Jews continued to face persecution despite the Enlightenment's emphasis on reason over tradition.

By the late 18th century many Central European Jews had been pushed further east into Galicia, a region encompassing parts of modern Poland and Ukraine. In the Russian Empire, Jewish populations were also beginning to be cordoned off, pushed further west into the Pale of the Settlement. These new Jewish migrants to the regions that today encompass part of Poland, Lithuania, Belarus, Ukraine, and Moldova, did not find themselves among sympathetic neighbors.

Jews who were forced into the Pale by the Russian Empire and those who were compelled to move into Galicia by the Habsburg Empire, who had annexed the region in 1772, were frequently victims of attacks by Cossacks, Ruthenians, and other hostile groups. While new Enlightenment principles may have been sweeping the courts and salons of Central Europe at this time, this wasn't the prevailing reality in the parts of Eastern Europe where Jews were forced to settle.

At this time of the Habsburg's annexation of Galicia, somewhere between 150,000 and 200,000 Jews were already living there (*Galicia*, n.d.). This number represented a significant percentage of the worldwide Jewish population, estimated to have been no more than 400,000 by the mid-18th century (*Historical Jewish Population*, 2024).

The larger region, the Pale, was created by Imperial Russia when Jewish merchants from Belorussia, a territory annexed from Poland in 1772, gained the ire of local business owners. They were having difficulty competing with Jewish businesses and wanted them out. The government of Empress Catherine II complied, banishing Jewish merchants from conducting business within the Russian Empire proper by 1790, setting the precedent for the creation of a special region that came to be known as the Pale of Settlement, the bounds of which were defined in 1804, and again in 1835 (*Pale of Settlement*, n.d.).

This legislation defined the areas on the fringe of the Empire where Jews were allowed to live and do business. While these populations of Russian Jews were free to move between the Pale and the neighboring Kingdom of Poland, they were not permitted to enter the territory of the Russian Empire itself (*Pale of Settlement*, n.d.). This period saw the continuation of restrictive laws against Jews across Central and Eastern Europe, limiting their rights to property, profession, and public worship, reinforcing their status as outsiders within European society.

By the time the 19th century swept in, as nations coalesced around emerging national identities, the enduring anti-Semitism of centuries past took on a more racial character. By 1857, the population of Jews in Galicia had increased substantially to 450,000 (*Galicia*, n.d.). The poor, agrarian Jews of Eastern Europe in Galicia, the Kingdom of Poland, and the Pale continued to face violence. Many attempted to go west to Central Europe but were often faced with restrictive measures. Some had luck in England and the United States. By the late 19th century, Russian Jews from the Pale attempting to settle in Germany were met with harsh resistance (*Historical Jewish Population*, 2024). Pseudo-scientific theories of racial hierarchy, which posited Jews as inferior, were growing, further entrenching existing prejudices and keeping large populations of Jews outside the physical borders and the business, cultural, and intellectual spaces of Western Europe.

The term "anti-Semitism" came into use for the first time in 1879 when a German journalist and activist named Wilhelm Marr saw the emerging wave of hate, violence, and prejudice against Jews in Central Europe, and decided that it was so fundamentally different from the kinds of maltreatment that the Jews had historically been subject to that it warranted a new term. The key difference between this new type of discrimination and the persecution that Jews had experienced previously was the racial aspect, and Marr's new term, using the word "Semitic" to describe a populace with origins in the Levant, rightly noted the discriminatory, racialist elements at play. This new form of hate targeted Jews because of their supposedly "inferior" biological characteristics, a deeply troubling notion, yet telling of the things to come in the 20th century.

Fascism in Europe

Italian Journalist and provocateur Benito Mussolini founded the Fascist Party in 1919. Capitalizing on the dissatisfaction of war veterans and economic turmoil in the wake of the First World War, Mussolini and his Blackshirt thugs used violence and intimidation to snuff out political opposition.

In 1922, Mussolini's march on Rome forced the weak hand of the Italian king Vittorio Emmanuelle III to appoint him as prime minister, marking the beginning of Fascist rule in Italy. Mussolini's regime emphasized aggressive nationalism, the glorification of the state over the individual, and the dream of creating a new kind of Roman Empire, one which would be based on the suppression of political freedoms, control of the media, and the aggressive pursuit of territorial expansion.

The success of Fascism in Italy served as a model for a Viennese art-school dropout named Adolf Hitler, who formed the National Socialist German Workers' (NAZI) Party in Germany. The Nazis adapted Fascist principles to their ideology, which emphasized racial purity, anti-Semitism, and the desire for *Lebensraum* (living space) for the German people. This idea continued the notion of keeping Jews out of Western European physical spaces, as well as its social, cultural, and economic spheres.

The economic devastation of the Great Depression, the humiliation of the Treaty of Versailles, staggering inflation, and the failing liberal-democratic Weimar Republic created a fertile ground for Nazi propaganda to proliferate. Hitler's rise to power in 1933 marked the beginning of a regime that would lead Germany and the world into the most destructive war in human history, and the mass genocide known as the Holocaust.

The rise of Fascism in Europe during the interwar period is often attributed to economic hardship and societal fears, factors that called for a new political order promising stability, national glory, and the suppression of perceived threats from the left. Fascist movements exploited these conditions, using propaganda, political violence, and the manipulation of democratic institutions to gain and consolidate power. As during the previous periods we've examined, the Jews were again cast as the scapegoat for society's ills.

Nazi Racial Ideology

The Nazis propagated a racial myth that White Europeans were descended from Aryans, a Proto-Indo-European people from Ancient Persia and the

Indian subcontinent. Our modern understanding of genetics and population migrations over the past 3,000 years renders Nazi thinking incoherent. Therefore, it's difficult to assess the logic behind Nazi race theory, since it appears to have had strong undercurrents of fantasy and myth. This element of a-historicism and imagined revisionism makes it difficult to dissect the exact meaning of the Aryan racial theories in any serious way.

Logic notwithstanding, the theory put forward an idea that Germans and other White Central Europeans who supposedly had a pure Aryan lineage were a superior race and were destined to rule over other "lesser" races. Jews, along with Romani people, homosexuals, people with physical and mental disabilities, and several other minorities were deemed inferior and came to be seen as threats to the racial purity and security of the German people.

This ideology was institutionalized through laws and actions that systematically stripped Jews and other targeted groups of their rights, dignity, and, ultimately, their lives. The Nuremberg Laws of 1935 legally codified racial discrimination, prohibiting Jews from obtaining citizenship and barring them from marrying or even engaging in romantic relations of any kind with German citizens and related "pure" European races.

The establishment of the Nazi regime marked the beginning of a systematic campaign to eradicate Jewish culture, heritage, and lives from the entirety of Europe. This campaign was meticulously organized and executed, starting with tactics that had been used against the Jews for centuries, including social isolation, dispossession, and ghettoization, and then culminating in a new kind of horror: The industrialized mass murder of the Holocaust.

The Nazis used propaganda to spread their anti-Semitic ideology, indoctrinating the German population and dehumanizing their victims to justify their actions. The ideologies put forward in the propaganda were rooted in the Aryan myth and a perverted interpretation of Darwinian theory and eugenics which aimed to create a "racially pure" state. This led to the envisioning of what was called "The Final Solution," a plan to purge Europe of all Jews. The final solution, while ultimately unsuccessful, led to the murder of six million Jews, among millions of others who were also considered to be sub-human by the Nazis.

The legacy of the Nazi regime and its ideologies of racial hatred extends beyond the immediate aftermath of World War II and serves as a cautionary tale of the dangers of dehumanization and racial prejudice. The world's response to the Nazi's atrocities and the horrors of World War II included the establishment of the UN in 1945 and the Nuremberg trials, which began that same year and fought to bring Nazis to justice.

The rise of Hitler's regime and the destruction brought by his racialized vision shows us the need for continued vigilance and education to combat anti-Semitism, hatred against other minorities, and violence against disabled people. The lessons learned from the atrocity of the Holocaust should be used instead to promote understanding and tolerance among people worldwide.

Ghettos, Concentration Camps, and Resistance

The re-establishment of ghettos during World War II by the Nazis was just one of the many inhumane and dehumanizing aspects of the Holocaust. The new ghettos erected by the Nazis across Europe were far from the traditional Jewish ghettos found in many European cities before the war. While it would be problematic to say that one form of ghettoization is more permissible than another, these new ghettos that emerged in Eastern Europe were specifically designed not just for segregation, but for on-site oppression and punishment and eventual deportation to concentration and extermination camps.

Ghettos were established in countries occupied by the Nazis all across the continent, including Poland, the Soviet Union (present-day Belarus, Ukraine, Lithuania, Latvia, and Russia), Czechoslovakia, Hungary, and Romania. These new, more grim, and misery-stricken ghettos were often constructed quickly after the German military occupation of these areas.

One of the first, largest, and most infamous ghettos was the Warsaw Ghetto in Poland. First established by Nazi Germany in October 1940, at its peak, the Warsaw Ghetto housed over 400,000 Jews, leading to overcrowded and inhumane living conditions (*Warsaw Ghetto*, 2024). The area, which covered barely more than a square mile, was surrounded by a wall topped with barbed wire and was closely guarded from escape attempts.

In the Soviet Union, ghettos were established following the German invasion in 1941. Cities such as Lviv, which was an important hub for Eastern European Jews in Galicia, Vilnius, which was a place of refuge for Jews under the Polish and Lithuanian Commonwealth, and Minsk, which was also a place where Jewish populations living in the Pale of Settlement sought refuge in the mid-19th century, became places of devastation. In each of these cities where Jewish life and communities once thrived, ghettos were erected and became places where thousands of Jews were confined before being deported or killed.

In Hungary, a country that had historically been somewhat tolerant of its assimilated Jewish populations from the Middle Ages up through the 19th century, things quickly fell apart. Following the German occupation in March 1944, ghettos were rapidly established in major cities and towns, where Jews were gathered before being deported to Auschwitz and other camps.

The conditions in the new ghettos of Europe were dire. Overcrowding, starvation, disease, and brutality were everyday realities for the inhabitants. The Nazis severely restricted food supplies, and sanitation was nonexistent, leading to outbreaks of contagious diseases. Many died from disease, starvation, and exposure to cold. Despite these devastatingly brutal conditions, many Jewish communities tried to maintain a semblance of cultural and religious life within the ghettos. Secret schools, religious services, and cultural events were held, even under the threat of death.

Acts of resistance and survival within the ghettos varied from armed uprisings, such as the Warsaw Ghetto uprising in April 1943, to more subtle forms of resistance, like smuggling food, medicine, and information. These ghettos, while initially serving as a means to control and segregate the Jewish population, became centers of Jewish resistance against the Nazi regime.

The creation and operation of these ghettos across Europe were a key part of the Nazis' systematic dehumanization campaign and the "final solution" it aimed for. The ghettos were just the first stop for many Jews who were deported from the countries they were living in as they were subsequently sent through an even more horrifying system of concentration camps that would come to symbolize the Holocaust's brutality. The camps were facilities specifically designed for the detention, forced labor, and mass murder of Jews, political prisoners, and others considered undesirable by the Nazi regime.

The concentration camp system expanded rapidly after the invasion of Poland in 1939, with camps like Auschwitz, Treblinka, and Sobibor becoming infamous for their roles in the implementation of the "final solution." Life in the camps was characterized by unimaginable cruelty. Prisoners were subjected to arbitrary violence, forced into grueling labor, and lived in inhumane conditions. Starvation, disease, and the constant threat of death were everyday realities.

Resistance within these camps, while more difficult due to the harsh conditions and strict surveillance, did occur. Acts of sabotage, secret religious observances, and even armed uprisings, such as the 1943 revolt at Sobibor and the 1944 uprising at Auschwitz, highlighted Jewish prisoners' dedication to their strong ethical and moral principles, even under great duress, and their stubborn refusal to allow the dehumanization to be perpetuated despite the Nazis' best efforts.

Like the ghettos, the camps were spread across the occupied territories, including Poland, Germany, Austria, and parts of the Soviet Union that were under German control. The establishment and liberation of these individual camps spanned the entire duration of World War II, from the early 1940s until the war's end in 1945, marking a period of systematic and industrialized murder that was unprecedented in human history. In the camps that were successfully liberated, Allied soldiers witnessed horrors of an indescribable magnitude.

The world was shocked at what they saw, from twisted eugenics experiments to mass starvation to the gas chambers to piles of bodies in the open air, mass graves with men women, and children all piled up on top of each other. Among the travesty and human suffering, there were rail-thin, often deathly ill survivors who had been starved. They bore the scars not just of their serial number tattoos, but of all the horrors they had witnessed. Many of these survivors carry these emotional wounds, as well as the tattooed numbers to this day; by the latest count, there are close to a quarter of a million survivors still living today (*Almost 80 Years after the Holocaust, 245,000 Jewish Survivors Are Still Alive*, 2024).

The Holocaust, Jewish Identity, and Post-War Justice

The Holocaust's profound impact on Jewish identity and the post-war justice efforts in the aftermath of World War II serve as telling chapters in understanding the wake of this tragic period, and how identity and attitudes among Jewish people around the world have been informed today.

The horrors of the holocaust remain a defining element in Jewish identity, especially among American and Israeli Jews. A 2013 Pew Research Center survey highlighted that 73% of American Jews consider remembering the Holocaust as an essential part of their Jewish identity, comparable in importance to leading an ethical life (*Chapter 3: Jewish Identity*, 2013).

This sentiment isn't confined to American Jews. In Israel, the Holocaust is deeply tied in with Jewish national identity, serving as a constant, not-so-distant reminder of the persecution faced by Jews throughout history, and as justification for the need for the continuation of a Jewish state in Palestine to serve as a sanctuary for Israeli citizens and Jews all over the world.

Post-War Justice: The Nuremberg Trials

In the aftermath of World War II, the Allied powers initiated the Nuremberg Trials as a means to bring Nazi war criminals and collaborators to justice. The trials, which were held from 1945 to 1946, introduced a new set of principles of international law concerning war crimes and crimes against humanity. The trials sought to hold individual Nazi officials accountable for their actions and aimed to establish a legal precedent for prosecuting the types of atrocities witnessed during the Holocaust, many of which were unprecedented in modern times due to their scope, scale, and level of brutality.

The trials indicted 24 high-ranking military and political officials of Nazi Germany, assessing their roles in war crimes, crimes against humanity, and the genocide that had engulfed Europe. The International Military Tribunal (IMT) provided a platform for presenting extensive evidence of Nazi atrocities, meticulously documenting the evidence of genocide, including the systemic murder of six million Jews. This was a groundbreaking effort in legal history, setting precedents for how the international community would seek to hold individuals accountable for violations of international law.

The pursuit of justice, however, did not conclude with the Nuremberg Trials. Many high-ranking Nazis escaped the reach of justice, either by fleeing or by committing suicide, as Adolf Hitler and Heinrich Himmler, the commander of the *Schutzstaffel* (or SS, Hitler's personal bodyguard unit) did.

The fact that numerous high-ranking officers successfully fled to other countries left a sense of unfinished business, as not all who were responsible for the Holocaust were held accountable. Despite some culpable Nazis having evaded international programs dedicated to tracking them down, efforts to recover and bring Nazi war criminals to justice continue to this day.

Aside from attempting to bring justice, the Nuremberg Trials and continued efforts to track down Nazi criminals to justice serve as a public acknowledgment of the sufferings endured by Holocaust victims. The pursuit of justice through the trials and subsequent efforts provides some semblance of closure to some survivors, but for others, the wounds will never be healed.

Before We Move On

As we close this chapter, and with the painful memories of the Holocaust etched indelibly into our collective consciousness, we must carry forward the responsibility to bear witness, to remember, and to ensure such atrocities never happen again. It's our duty, from armchair historians up to academics to learn something from history, to recognize the signs of rising hatred and intolerance, and to stand firmly against them when we see patterns repeat themselves.

Looking ahead, we'll explore the early years of Israel following the War of Independence, looking at how today's Israeli attitudes and culture were born from the ashes of the Holocaust. We'll delve into Israel's persistent struggle for recognition, its triumphs in building a homeland for the Jewish people, and how its establishment marked the beginning of a new saga in Jewish history.

Chapter 11: Israel and the Middle East

How does a nascent nation survive amid continuous threats from hostile neighbors? Israel's formative years were a period marked by a substantial influx of immigrants, intense Arab-Israeli conflicts, and pivotal social and political transformations. Through mass immigration, wars, and peace efforts, we see the complex dynamics that have come to inform contemporary Israel arise.

Mass Immigration and Early Statehood

The establishment of Israel in 1948 and the subsequent wave of mass immigration drastically shaped its demographic and cultural landscape. The fledgling Jewish state faced the immense challenge of integrating a vast influx of immigrants from various backgrounds, including Holocaust survivors from Europe and Jewish communities from Arab countries under the shadow of ongoing conflict.

This era was pivotal in forming Israel's diverse society, which endures to this day, blending languages, traditions, and cultures into a unique patchwork of modern Hebrew culture that laid the groundwork for the nation's social and political fabric.

Modern Hebrew language, revitalized as the nation's lingua franca, didn't just serve as a new means of communication but was also a symbol of unity and renewal for many who had endured the Holocaust's horrors. The re-introduction of Hebrew as a modern, spoken language dates back only to the late 19th century, and was recognized as the official language of Jews in Palestine by 1922.

Ben-Yehuda's vision for Modern Hebrew involved transforming Biblical Hebrew, previously used only in study, into a living language for everyday use. He was inspired by European nationalist movements and saw Hebrew as crucial for Jewish nationalism. Despite the inherent challenges in creating a modern language from an ancient one, including the substantial opposition he met from ultra-Orthodox communities, Ben-Yehuda's dedication to the ideological principles behind Modern Hebrew laid the foundation for the language's resurgence.

Through this kind of cultural nationalism, cultural festivals, educational reforms, and public discourse, Israel was successful in cultivating a unique national culture. This new culture embraced the heritage of its immigrant population from the Diaspora and welcomed them into the fold by encouraging integration into it. This was how the Israeli state was successful in forging a shared sense of identity and destiny amidst the challenges of a pluralistic Jewish population and dealt with the clashes between factions within Zionism and the newly-founded Israeli state, a factor that would come into play once the heated conflict between Israel and its neighbors broke out.

The War of 1948

The Israeli War of Independence began as soon as Israeli statehood was declared on May 14, 1948. The declaration of the independent state, which was recognized swiftly by major powers like the United States and the Soviet Union, fulfilled the Zionist aspiration for a Jewish state but also plunged the region into a new phase of conflict. The newly declared state found itself immediately under attack by its five neighboring Arab states—Egypt, Syria, Lebanon, Jordan, and Iraq, with additional support from Saudi Arabia and Yemen.

Amid all this, Israel had already been in the throes of absorbing a massive wave of Jewish immigrants from all over the world. These new arrivals, fleeing the aftermath of World War II and the Holocaust, sought refuge and a new beginning in their ancestral homeland. The challenges they faced once they arrived in the newly-formed nation were monumental, as they had to integrate into a society that was just coming together, and was now under siege. As soon as conflict broke out, it became apparent that internal divisions lay within the Zionist movement, and the challenges of unifying various armed groups under a single national military command were daunting, to say the least.

Israeli forces faced off against Arab militias led by Haj Amin al-Husseini in Jerusalem. As the Grand Mufti, he became the de facto military commander of the Palestinian resistance in the Holy City. Meanwhile, conflicts were brewing internally between the newly-created Israeli Defense Force (IDF) and a Zionist militia group called the Irgun. Led by Menachem Begin, the group sought to import arms through a cargo ship named the Altalena. David Ben-Gurion, Israel's prime minister intervened, giving orders that the ship be stopped at all costs. This led to a direct engagement between the IDF and the Irgun, who were supposed to have been absorbed by the IDF by that point. This friendly-fire incident between Israeli factions led to the death of 82 people ("Israel - Immigration and Conflict," 2020).

Despite the conflicts between the IDF and smaller Zionist militias such as the Irgun, and being outnumbered and lacking in heavy arms, the Israeli forces managed to come out on top, even expanding their territorial holdings beyond the UN Partition Plan's allocations, capturing parts of what was still at the time Mandated Palestine. These areas included Galilee, Jezreel Valley, Negev, West Jerusalem, and parts of Palestine's coastal plain.

The swift victory, however thrilling for the young Israeli state, came at a massive cost that would come to plague them for decades. The territorial grab and the forced removal of Arab Palestinians led to a massive displacement that endures today and remains the primary factor that has fueled the Israeli-Palestinian conflict. Through making a significant percentage of Arab Palestinians displaced refugees, the war upped the stakes for a Palestinian-Israeli conflict which had already been brewing over tensions from Zionist mass migration.

The resolution of the war failed to bring peace to the region, but what the armistice agreements of 1949 accomplished was to cement Israel's territorial gains, enlarging Israel's size by about one-third compared to the initial UN proposal. As it stood after the armistice agreement, Israel's footprint covered roughly 78% of what was once Mandated Palestine (*1948 Palestine War*, 2024).

The expansion realized by the young state of Israel marked the beginning of what would become a new, drawn-out struggle over land, identity, and sovereignty that would ripple throughout the region. The result was a dynamic in which Israel was constantly at odds with its neighbors, a dynamic that endures today.

Historical Timeline of Arab-Israeli Conflicts

This timeline is not complete, and Arab-Israeli conflicts have been frequent. However, it hints at the immense regional difficulties even with the specific Israeli-Palestinian question put to the side.

- **1948: War of Independence**
  - **Countries Involved:** Israel against Egypt, Jordan, Lebanon, Syria, Iraq, Palestinian Arab forces, Saudi Arabia, and Yemen.
  - **Result:** Israeli territorial expansion.
- **1956: Suez Crisis**
  - **Countries Involved:** Israel, the UK, and France against Egypt.
  - **Result:** Egypt retained control of the Suez Canal.
- **1967: Six-Day War**
  - **Countries Involved:** Israel against Egypt, Jordan, Syria, and Iraq. Some US naval reinforcement in the Straits of Tiran, but no direct engagement with Egypt.

- **Result:** Israeli territorial expansion through the occupation of Egypt's Sinai Peninsula.
- **1973: Yom Kippur War**
  - **Countries Involved:** Israel against Egypt and Syria.
  - **Result:** Led to the first peace talks and the Camp David Accords of 1979.
- **1982: Lebanon War**
  - **Countries Involved:** Israel against the Palestine Liberation Organization (PLO) operating in Lebanon, with Syrian involvement.
  - **Result:** Israeli occupation of Southern Lebanon.
- **2006: Second Lebanon War**
  - **Countries Involved:** Israel against Hezbollah in Lebanon.
  - **Result:** UN-brokered ceasefire.

Peace Processes

1979: The Camp David Accords

In 1979, the Camp David Accords became a milestone achievement in Middle Eastern politics. For the first time, Egypt officially recognized Israel's existence, becoming the first Arab country to do so. Orchestrated by U.S. President Jimmy Carter, this peace agreement was the result of 12 days of intense negotiations at Camp David. The Accords comprised two framework agreements: one that laid the groundwork for the Egyptian-Israeli peace treaty, and another that proposed a framework for broader peace throughout the region, including Palestinian autonomy in the West Bank and Gaza.

The signing of the Camp David Accords shifted the geopolitical landscape of the region. It led to the return of the Sinai Peninsula to Egypt, a territory that had been captured by Israel during the Six-Day War in 1967, in exchange for Egypt's concession and the normalization of diplomatic and commercial relations. This agreement demonstrated the potential for peace through diplomacy and set a precedent for future Arab-Israeli negotiations. The Accords' success and limitations continue to be a reference point in ongoing Middle Eastern peace processes.

1993: The Oslo Accords

The Oslo Accords of 1993 represented another hopeful moment in relations between Israel and the Palestinians. Staged in secrecy in Norway, these behind-closed-doors negotiations carried out on neutral ground brought about the first direct diplomacy between Israel and the Palestine Liberation Organization (PLO).

The Accords were successful in establishing mutual recognition between Israel and Palestine for the first time, leading to the creation of the Palestinian Authority (PA), a governing authority that would hold sway in certain parts of the West

Bank and Gaza. The hope was that this meeting could pave the way for a comprehensive peace agreement, one that would address issues such as ever-encroaching Israeli settlements in the West Bank, the status of Jerusalem, and the borders of a future Palestinian state.

Despite the signs of progress and hope the Oslo meetings inspired, the peace process encountered numerous challenges, leading to fluctuating tensions and ongoing negotiations in the pursuit of a lasting resolution.

1994: The Israel-Jordan Peace Treaty

The Israel-Jordan Peace Treaty, signed in 1994, ended the state of war between Israel and Jordan and established mutual diplomatic relations. This treaty was brokered with the help of the United States, further contributing to the building momentum for peace in the Middle East.

The agreement included provisions on border security, water sharing, and cooperation in tourism and environmental protection. This landmark treaty helped normalize relations between the two countries while opening diplomatic channels for future peace negotiations.

Recent Peace Negotiations

Recent efforts in Middle Eastern peace processes have focused on addressing longstanding issues through negotiation and international diplomacy.

These include some attempts to renew Israeli-Palestinian peace talks. However, the most notable breakthroughs have been between Israel and other Arab states. In 2020, U.S. President Donald Trump hosted the signing of the "Abraham Accords," wherein both the U.A.E. and Bahrain normalized relations with Israel. Sudan and Morocco joined suit shortly after.

Despite ever-present challenges and Israel's ongoing assault on Gaza following the October 7, 2023, Hamas attack on Israel, there is now ample precedent for sustained dialogue and cooperation among all parties. To what extent Israel's invasion of Gaza and its accompanying humanitarian crisis affects future attempts at peace is up in the air. Moreover, international pressure on Israel for a ceasefire is growing. At the time of this book's publishing, both major U.S. political parties are split, with prominent members in each affirming Israel's right to self-defense while others clamor for a ceasefire.

Israeli Social, Economic, and Political Developments

As Israel navigates through the 21st century, its presence as the only democracy in the region is marked by the substantial progress it has made since the days of its founding. These cultural, social, economic, and political transformations aren't just isolated factors, but are closely interconnected, giving us a nuanced picture of a modern nation-state that is both traditional and innovative.

Social Progress and Inclusivity

Israel's social landscape thrives today and is distinguished by the confluence of cultures brought by immigrants from countries all over the world. This melting pot has created a rich diversity of Jewish communities, alongside significant Arab, Druze, and other ethnic minorities, each contributing unique cultural and religious traditions. Challenges arise in managing this diversity, particularly in balancing the secular and religious elements, addressing socioeconomic disparities, and integrating communities. Despite these issues, efforts towards social cohesion and equality continue to evolve, reflecting Israel's dynamic social fabric and its commitment to democracy.

Despite the inherent ethno-nationalistic principles of the Israeli State and militarization of its citizenry, who are all subject to compulsory military service, Israel boasts several progressive strides in recognizing and supporting the rights of many groups, cementing its global standing as a Western-style liberal democracy. This tolerant environment allows for freedom in social interactions and personal expression for all Israeli citizens, highlighting the country's commitment to individual rights and equality.

Arab citizens of Israel, both Islamic and Christian, constitute about 20% of the population and are subject to a mix of tolerance and discrimination within a state that defines itself as Jewish (Kopelwitz, 2023). While Arab Israelis enjoy full citizenship and rights, including representation in parliament, they still face socioeconomic disparities, with their communities often experiencing lower living standards and higher poverty rates compared to Jewish areas.

Despite the legal recognition of equality, some argue that indirect discrimination persists, as seen in funding disparities and access to services. Others point out that economic disparities are not necessarily the result of discrimination. Nevertheless, the reality of living as an Arab in Israel is marked by a struggle for identity and socioeconomic equality amid ongoing debates on how to organize a pluralistic society. It's the same struggle that continues in all Western democracies, but the situation in Israel is complicated by violence and unrest, highlighting the difficulties of Palestinians who hold Israeli citizenship.

The Israeli Economy

From its foundation in 1948, Israel has evolved from an economy reliant on agriculture and imports into a high-tech powerhouse, recognized globally for its innovation and technological advancements. This trajectory has been marked by strategic investments in research and development, a highly educated workforce, and an entrepreneurial culture that has encouraged startups and entrepreneurialism.

The technology sector is one of the points of pride in Israel's economic success story, contributing substantially to the country's GDP and positioning it as a leader in fields such as cybersecurity and medical and agricultural technology. This growing sector attracts foreign investment and has facilitated partnerships with multinational corporations. The Israeli government supports this growth through favorable policies, including tax incentives and funding for research and development.

Israel's tech industry faces a heavy amount of controversy, particularly regarding its role in developing and exporting sophisticated spyware and digital forensics tools. Some of these technologies have come under international scrutiny for their use in surveillance and intelligence gathering, practices that are often illegal or heavily regulated in Western countries. These tools are capable of violating the digital privacy of citizens in the countries where they're used, raising ethical and legal concerns about their deployment against journalists, activists, and political opponents both within and outside Israel. The global debate over data, surveillance, and individual privacy rights is intensified by these developments, positioning Israel at the center of complex discussions about the responsible use of technology in international espionage and cybersecurity.

Despite the impressive economic achievements since Israel's founding, the country frequently faces challenges, including regional instability, which necessitates considerable defense spending and causes internal socioeconomic disparities. The high cost of living and housing affordability are persistent concerns for many Israelis.

Recent Political Shifts in Israel

In recent years, Israel's political landscape has undergone a radical re-orientation characterized by a pronounced shift to the right. Key to this shift has been Prime Minister Benjamin Netanyahu and his Likud party, which have heavily shaped the nation's contemporary political discourse. Under Netanyahu's leadership, Likud has prioritized security concerns, continued West Bank settlements, and pushed a conservative fiscal policy, appealing to a broad constituency that values a strong stance against perceived external threats and supports a market-oriented economy.

Netanyahu's tenure has also been marked by challenges to the Israeli parliamentary system, particularly through attempts to alter the balance of power among Israel's governance institutions. Critics argue that some of these efforts undermine the independence of the judiciary and erode democratic checks and balances. This includes proposed legal reforms that would weaken the Supreme Court, raising concerns about the potential for increased executive power and its implications for Israeli democracy.

The shift to the right under Netanyahu and Likud reflects broader trends within Israeli society, where security concerns, religious and national identity, and economic policy preferences have driven electoral gains for right-wing parties. This political realignment has implications for Israel's domestic policy, especially regarding civil liberties and minority rights, as well as its foreign policy, particularly in relations with Palestinians and broader Middle Eastern dynamics.

Netanyahu has been criticized both in Israel and internationally for exacerbating divisions within Israeli society and between Israel and the international community. As Israel navigates complex internal challenges and external threats, the political direction set by Netanyahu and Likud continues to be a subject of scrutiny both on the domestic front and abroad, reflecting the ongoing evolution of Israeli politics in a rapidly changing regional and global context.

Israel's Global Influence

Israel's social, economic, and political developments have shaped its internal dynamics and also its position on the global stage. The country's technology, agriculture, and healthcare industries have established Israel as a significant player in international markets. These achievements reflect

Israel's emphasis on innovation and entrepreneurship, which have been central to its long-term economic strategy. On the environmental front, Israel's innovations in water conservation and renewable energy are contributing to global efforts to address climate change, showcasing how national initiatives can have wide-reaching international impacts.

Politically, Israel's strategic alliances, especially with the United States and Western Europe, have been important in its foreign policy and defense strategy. Israel's international relations paint a complex picture, however, mainly due to the possible targeting of Palestinian civilians in the war against Hamas. The climbing civilian casualties and the cutting off of international aid and resources to Gaza, aside from irking traditional allies such as the U.S., also affect normalization agreements with several Arab states. These agreements, part of the broader Abraham Accords, mark a significant shift in regional dynamics, and Israel's actions today threaten to unravel all the diplomatic efforts of the past.

Before We Move On

As we leave behind our discussion of Israel's standing in the Middle East and globally, it's now time to take a closer look at Jewish life around the world in the 21st century. The next chapter will guide us through contemporary Jewish identity, community dynamics, and the ongoing evolution of

Jewish life in a rapidly changing world. We'll look at how modern challenges and opportunities are shaping the practices, beliefs, and community relationships of the Jewish people today.

Chapter 12: Contemporary Jewish Life and Israel Today

As a river carves its path through the landscape, so does history shape a people's identity. Such is the ever-evolving story of Jewish life in the 21st century, where millennia of heritage meet the challenges and opportunities of a rapidly changing world.

Jews today stand at a unique crossroads where tradition intersects with modernity, prompting a reexamination of what it means to be Jewish. From the diversity within Jewish communities to the Palestinian question, it's first and foremost important to understand the contemporary issues and dynamics shaping Jewish life and their implications for the future. In many cases, issues such as the complexities of Jewish identity, tradition and historical narratives, power structures, social justice, and diplomacy and humanitarian concerns, all play a role in the nuanced and often polarizing discussions around key issues.

Jewish Identity and Community in the 21st Century

Jewish identity and community today reflect the rich heritage of the past and the challenges of the modern world. This evolution is influenced significantly by globalization, which has expanded the avenues through which Jewish identity is expressed and experienced.

Jewish identity today is not monolithic, but rather, is characterized by a diversity of thought, values, and beliefs that span cultural, religious, political, and secular dimensions. This diversity of levels of observance and political orientations shows how Jews have managed to maintain a cohesive identity through tradition despite vast differences and the geographic spread and varied socio-political contexts in which they find themselves.

Cultural aspects of Jewish identity today encompass a wide range of expressions, from traditional music and food to literature and art. These cultural markers serve as a means of preserving Jewish heritage and as a vehicle for engaging with the broader global community, showcasing the rich contributions of Jewish culture to the world.

The spectrum of Jewish religious belief and practice is broad, ranging from Orthodox to Reform movements, secular humanistic Judaism, and movements such as Workers Circle, which emphasize social justice more than religious practice. Each current Jewish identity offers a different approach to Jewish law, tradition, and modern life, reflecting the community's internal diversity and its response to contemporary challenges. The concept of *Tikkun Olam* (repairing the world) is an example of an idea that gets interpreted differently across the spectrum of Jewish thought, as it could represent a call for social action, environmental stewardship, protection of the Jewish homeland, or personal and spiritual self-improvement.

The secular dimension of Jewish identity highlights the importance of cultural and ethnic identity among those who may not actively participate in religious practices. For many, Israeli and American Jews in particular, Jewish identity is deeply intertwined with historical experiences, particularly the memory of the Holocaust, and the ongoing struggle for survival and self-determination in a more symbolic sense.

The role of technology and social media has been transformative in connecting Jewish communities globally, allowing for a shared space where individuals and groups can exchange ideas, celebrate traditions, and mobilize around common causes. This digital connectivity has also played an important role in confronting challenges such as widespread online anti-Semitism and conspiracy theories that target Jews.

The Palestinian Question and International Relations

The ongoing Israeli-Palestinian conflict continues to impact the region and international relations. Since war broke out between Israel and Hamas on October 7, 2023, the international community has been deeply concerned about the escalation and its implications.

In the wake of the October 7th attack, U.S. President Joe Biden initially expressed strong support for Israel, reinforcing the U.S.'s commitment to protecting Israel by sending arms shipments and moving warships closer to Israel. Since then, both Biden and Secretary of State Anthony Blinken have expressed frustration with Israel's unrelenting assault and the mounting humanitarian situation in Gaza. As mentioned previously, U.S. Vice President Kamala Harris has called for a ceasefire, underscoring the urgency of the crisis from a humanitarian perspective.

A UN expert and numerous international scholars of genocide have repeatedly flashed warning signs over Israel's campaign against Gaza. They fear it may meet the internationally recognized standard of ethnic cleansing (*UN Expert Warns of New Instance of Mass Ethnic Cleansing of Palestinians, Calls for Immediate Ceasefire*, 2023).

The United Nations Security Council has convened multiple emergency meetings but has failed to reach a consensus on the situation. To this date, the conflict has resulted in significant Palestinian civilian casualties, with the current overall death toll of Palestinians in Gaza now over 30,000 (Kim, 2024). On the Israeli side, more than 1,200 have perished (Picheta, 2024). On March 25, 2024, the Security Council passed a resolution demanding an immediate ceasefire for the remainder of Ramadan. However, the Israeli offensive continues.

Future Outlook and Challenges

The international Jewish community and Jews in Israel face a broad array of challenges and opportunities as they move into the future. These challenges include assimilation, anti-Semitism, and the preservation of cultural heritage, each of which plays a critical role in shaping their continuity and identity.

Assimilation has been a double-edged sword for Jewish communities worldwide. On one hand, it has allowed Jews to integrate into the broader societies they live within, allowing them to contribute to fields such as science, arts, and politics. On the other hand, assimilation poses a threat to Jewish cultural and religious traditions, potentially leading to a dilution of identity and practices. The challenge lies in navigating the balance between integration and the maintenance of distinct Jewish cultural and religious identity.

Anti-Semitism is set to remain a persistent threat into the future. While it may evolve in form, as we've seen throughout the pages of this book, persecution has consistently been the looming shadow following Jewish people as they make their way around the world. Recent years have seen a resurgence in anti-Semitic incidents globally, fueled by political extremism, economic uncertainty, and even COVID-19 conspiracy theories.

The resurgence of anti-Semitism worldwide isn't just a direct threat to the safety and well-being of Jews, but it also challenges the notion of whether the diverse and inclusive Western societies Jews live in are in fact as diverse and inclusive as they purport to be; an issue we also, unfortunately, see in Israel through the treatment of Israeli-Arab citizens and the ongoing assault on Gaza.

Maintaining cultural heritage in the face of globalization and changing societal norms represents yet another challenge for contemporary Jews. As the world becomes more interconnected, Jewish communities often need to seek out new, innovative ways to preserve their rich traditions and histories while also adapting to the changing landscape. This includes rethinking community structures, education, and direct engagement with both Jewish and non-Jewish populations.

Looking ahead, the future direction for Jewish communities is likely to be influenced by several factors, including global trends and evolving cultural and religious practices. Demographic shifts, such as the growth of Jewish populations in certain areas and declines in others, will likely necessitate new approaches to community building and public outreach. Additionally, evolving cultural elements will continue to reflect how Jewish people and communities identify with, understand, and live out their Jewish identities.

In navigating these challenges, the Jewish community is poised to continue its long history of adaptation and success in the face of oppression. By valuing diversity, pursuing social justice worldwide, embracing innovation, and encouraging dialogues between those both inside and outside the Jewish world, there is a path forward that honors the past while boldly stepping into the future.

Conclusion

From the ancient roots of Jews in the Holy Land to the complexities of contemporary Jewish life and the modern State of Israel, throughout this narrative, we've witnessed the resilience of the Jewish people, their enduring spirit, and the richness of their cultural and religious identity. Almost miraculously, these have evolved yet remained distinct across centuries and continents.

Concerns about the well-being of Palestinian communities have recently highlighted the ongoing challenges in achieving lasting peace in the Levant. This deeply troubling moment in history serves as a reminder of the importance of striving for peace, understanding, and coexistence not just in the Middle East but around the world.

The narrative of the Jewish people is far from complete. As new chapters unfold, they will undoubtedly face continued challenges, but in those challenges, they will also find opportunities for growth, dialogue, and reconciliation.

Carry forward the lessons learned from this book into your life and the communities and spaces you engage with. By having conversations that bridge divides, advocating for justice, and supporting efforts toward peace, we all can contribute to a future that honors the legacy of the Jewish people and the well-being of all peoples around the globe.

In closing, let's take a moment to reflect on the power that history has to inform our present and inspire our future actions. May the resilience, innovation, and spirit of community that has characterized Jewish life through the ages guide us toward a more inclusive, just, and peaceful world.

L'chaim! (to life).

Note to the Reader

Sharing sincere feedback is the best way to support (and improve) the work of independent publishers. If you enjoyed and found value in this book, please leave a review and invite others to learn about and reflect upon our common past to build a promising future.

Scan the code to leave a review!

References

A Brief Introduction to Hasidism. (2019). PBS.
https://www.pbs.org/alifeapart/intro.html

A century of immigration, 1820-1924 - from haven to home: 350 years of jewish life in america. (2019). Library of Congress.
https://www.loc.gov/exhibits/haventohome/haven-century.html

Abrahamic religions. (2024, January 31). Wikipedia.
https://en.wikipedia.org/w/index.php?title=Abrahamic_religions&oldid=1201522656

Age of enlightenment. (2019, January 13). Wikipedia.
https://en.wikipedia.org/wiki/Age_of_Enlightenment

Alexander, J. C. (2006). The Jewish question. *Oxford University Press EBooks*, 459–502.
https://doi.org/10.1093/acprof:oso/9780195162509.003.0035

Aliyah. (2024, January 22). Wikipedia.
https://en.wikipedia.org/w/index.php?title=Aliyah&oldid=1197808937

Almost 80 years after the Holocaust, 245,000 Jewish survivors are still alive. (2024, January 23). AP News.
https://apnews.com/article/holocaust-survivors-numbers-report-claims-conference-890c9ad6aa7bc1cf99e1cbe40e61c013

American Jewish Committee. (2023, November 1). *Timeline: Key events in the israel-arab and Israeli-Palestinian conflict.* American Jewish Committee.
https://www.ajc.org/IsraelConflictTimeline

American Jewish committee urges social media firms to confront antisemitism on platforms. (2023, February 21). American Jewish Committee.
https://www.ajc.org/news/american-jewish-committee-urges-social-media-firms-to-confront-antisemitism-on-platforms

Ammann, S. (2022). *The fall of Jerusalem: Cultural trauma as a process.* de Gruyter Open Access.

https://www.degruyter.com/document/doi/10.1515/o
pth-2022-0212/html

Ancient and modern art. (n.d.). Jewish Virtual Library.
https://www.jewishvirtuallibrary.org/art

Anti-Defamation League. (2013). *A brief history of anti-*
semitism.
https://www.adl.org/sites/default/files/documents/as
sets/pdf/education-outreach/Brief-History-on-Anti-
Semitism-A.pdf

Anti-Semitism and Jewish views on discrimination. (2021,
May 11). Pew Research Center's Religion & Public Life
Project.
https://www.pewresearch.org/religion/2021/05/11/a
nti-semitism-and-jewish-views-on-discrimination/

Antisemitism in History: Nazi antisemitism. (2019).
United States Holocaust Memorial Museum.
https://encyclopedia.ushmm.org/content/en/article/a
ntisemitism-in-history-nazi-antisemitism

Arab-Israeli wars | history, conflict, & facts. (2019). In
Encyclopædia Britannica.
https://www.britannica.com/event/Arab-Israeli-wars

Arab-Israeli wars summary. (n.d.). Encyclopedia
Britannica. Retrieved May 15, 2021, from
https://www.britannica.com/summary/Arab-Israeli-
wars

Babylonian captivity. (2024, February 2). Wikipedia.
https://en.wikipedia.org/w/index.php?title=Babyloni
an_captivity&oldid=1202402028

Background & overview of Orthodox Judaism. (2019).
Jewish Virtual Library.
https://www.jewishvirtuallibrary.org/background-
and-overview-of-orthodox-judaism

Bamford, T. (2020, November 17). *The Nuremberg trial*
and its legacy. The National WWII Museum.
https://www.nationalww2museum.org/war/articles/t
he-nuremberg-trial-and-its-legacy

Barr, J. (1985). The question of religious influence: The
case of Zoroastrianism, Judaism, and Christianity.
Journal of the American Academy of Religion, 53(2),
201–235. https://www.jstor.org/stable/1464919

Baskind, S. (n.d.). *An introduction to Jewish art in the United States Before 1900*. Smart History. Retrieved February 6, 2024, from https://smarthistory.org/an-introduction-to-jewish-art-in-the-united-states-before-1900/

Beegle, D. M. (2017). Moses. In *Encyclopædia Britannica*. https://www.britannica.com/biography/Moses-Hebrew-prophet

Beginnings of the golden age in Spain. (2011, April 28). JewishHistory.org. https://www.jewishhistory.org/golden-age-in-spain/

Belmaker, G. (2014, March 26). *Jerusalem history: The first and second temples*. Moon Travel Guides. https://www.moon.com/travel/arts-culture/jerusalem-history-first-second-temples/

Bennett, A. (2021, February 10). *Rome & Jerusalem: The historical context of Jesus Christ*. TheCollector. https://www.thecollector.com/jesus-christ-in-context-rome-jerusalem-judea/

Berenbaum, M. (2018). Anti-Semitism | history, facts, & examples. In *Encyclopædia Britannica*. https://www.britannica.com/topic/anti-Semitism

Berenbaum, M. (2019). Anti-Semitism in medieval Europe. In *Encyclopædia Britannica*. https://www.britannica.com/topic/anti-Semitism/Anti-Semitism-in-medieval-Europe

Berlin, A. (2011). *Forced Conversion in The Oxford dictionary of the Jewish religion*. Oxford University Press. https://www.oxfordreference.com/display/10.1093/acref/9780199730049.001.0001/acref-9780199730049-e-0734

Bix, A. S. (2020). "Remember the Sabbath": a history of technological decisions and innovation in Orthodox Jewish communities. *History and Technology*, 1–35. https://doi.org/10.1080/07341512.2020.1816339

Brazil virtual Jewish history tour. (n.d.). Jewish Virtual Library. https://www.jewishvirtuallibrary.org/brazil-virtual-jewish-history-tour

Bronze age. (2024, February 5). Wikipedia. https://en.wikipedia.org/w/index.php?title=Bronze Age&oldid=1203552643

Brown, W. (2017, October 25). *Early Judaism.* World History Encyclopedia. https://www.worldhistory.org/article/1139/early-judaism/

Brown, Wi. (2017, July 13). *Ancient Israelite & Judean religion.* World History Encyclopedia. https://www.worldhistory.org/article/1097/ancient-israelite--judean-religion/

Byzantine Empire. (n.d.). Jewish Virtual Library. https://www.jewishvirtuallibrary.org/byzantine-empire

Cataliotti, J. (n.d.). *Maccabean revolt causes, aftermath & significance.* Study.com. https://study.com/academy/lesson/maccabean-revolt-overview-history.html

Causes of the Jewish war against the Romans. (n.d.). Josephus. Retrieved February 5, 2024, from https://josephus.org/causesOfWar.htm

Center for Preventive Action. (2023, December 4). *Israeli-Palestinian conflict.* Global Conflict Tracker: Council on Foreign Relations. https://www.cfr.org/global-conflict-tracker/conflict/israeli-palestinian-conflict

Chaim Weizmann. (2024, February 24). Wikipedia. https://en.wikipedia.org/w/index.php?title=Chaim Weizmann&oldid=1210055844

Chapter 3: Jewish Identity. (2013, October 1). Pew Research Center's Religion & Public Life Project. https://www.pewresearch.org/religion/2013/10/01/chapter-3-jewish-identity/

Chapter 3: The ancient Israelites. (n.d.). In *San Pasqual Union District School.* Retrieved February 5, 2024, from https://www.sanpasqualunion.net/cms/lib/CA01000408/Centricity/Domain/69/6th%20Textbook/chap03.pdf

Clark, R. (2005). Moses Mendelssohn's approach to Jewish integration in light of his reconciliation of traditional judaism and enlightenment rationalism. In *Cedarville*

University.
https://digitalcommons.cedarville.edu/cgi/viewconte
nt.cgi?article=1207&context=history_and_governmen
t_publications
Colgan, L. (n.d.). *A way of life. Why is the Talmud*
important to Jews? Żydowski Instytut Historyczny.
https://www.jhi.pl/en/articles/a-way-of-life-why-is-
the-talmud-important-to-jews
Conservative Judaism. (2024, January 3). Wikipedia.
https://en.wikipedia.org/w/index.php?title=Conserva
tive_Judaism&oldid=1193456225
Conversion history: Talmudic period. (n.d.). My Jewish
Learning. Retrieved February 5, 2024, from
https://www.myjewishlearning.com/article/conversio
n-history-talmudic-period/
Coordinator, C. (n.d.). *Historic and cultural interactions*
between Islam and Judaism, Muslims and Jews .
CPNN: Culture of Peace News Network. https://cpnn-
world.org/new/?p=16396
Culture and religion: Judaism. (n.d.). In *Office of*
Multicultural Affairs.
https://tfhc.nt.gov.au/_data/assets/pdf_file/0016/2
52223/nt-judaism-fact-sheet.pdf
Daily life in the ghettos – The holocaust explained:
Designed for schools. (1933, January 30). The
Holocaust Explained.
https://www.theholocaustexplained.org/the-
camps/ghettos-an-overview/daily-life-in-the-ghettos/
Danahy, K. (2023, November 21). *Tribe of Judah in the*
Bible. Study.com.
https://study.com/academy/lesson/tribe-of-judah-
history-descendants.html
Darby, E. (n.d.). *The archaeology of Jerusalem*. Bible
Odyssey. Retrieved February 5, 2024, from
https://blog.bibleodyssey.net/articles/the-
archaeology-of-jerusalem/
David, A. (2023, October 9). In first, archaeologists extract
DNA of ancient Israelites. *Haaretz*.
https://www.haaretz.com/archaeology/2023-10-
09/ty-article/in-first-archaeologists-extract-dna-of-
ancient-israelites/

Davies, P. (2019). Dead sea scrolls. In *Encyclopædia Britannica*. https://www.britannica.com/topic/Dead-Sea-Scrolls

Dead sea scrolls. (2024, January 28). Wikipedia. https://en.wikipedia.org/w/index.php?title=Dead_Sea_Scrolls&oldid=1199911430

Denova, R. (2022, January 31). *Sadducees*. World History Encyclopedia. https://www.worldhistory.org/Sadducees/

Dershowitz, A. M. (1977). *The vanishing American Jew*. The New York Times. https://archive.nytimes.com/www.nytimes.com/books/first/d/dershowitz-jew.html?scp=22&sq=israel+conversion&st=cse

Destruction of the second temple in 70 CE. (n.d.). Harvard Divinity School. https://rpl.hds.harvard.edu/faq/destruction-second-temple-70-ce

Dospěl, M. (2017, August 7). *The four-room house: Typically israelite?* Biblical Archaeology Society. https://www.biblicalarchaeology.org/daily/archaeology-today/biblical-archaeology-topics/four-room-house-typically-israelite/

Drake Boehm, B., & Holcomb, M. (2020). *Jews and the arts in medieval Europe*. Metmuseum.org. https://www.metmuseum.org/toah/hd/jewm/hd_jewm.htm

Drane, J. (n.d.). *Four differences between Canaanite religion and Israel's faith*. Mennonite Brethren Collegiate Institute. https://www.mbci.mb.ca/site/assets/files/1181/four_differences_between_canaanite_religion.pdf

Duignan, B. (2018). Enlightenment. In *Encyclopedia Britannica*. https://www.britannica.com/event/Enlightenment-European-history

Economy of Israel. (2024, February 5). Wikipedia. https://en.wikipedia.org/w/index.php?title=Economy_of_Israel&oldid=1203634969

Einhorn, D., Raphall, M. J., Phillips, E., Michelbacher, M. J., Levy, I., Leeser, I., Mordechai, A., Lincoln, A.,

Wales, J. A., Wise, S., Meccler, D. L., & Brenner, F. (2004, September 9). *From haven to home: 350 Years of Jewish life in America*. Library of Congress. https://www.loc.gov/exhibits/haventohome/haven-challenges.html

Eisen, R. (2011a). Modern Zionism. *The Peace and Violence of Judaism*, 141–204. https://doi.org/10.1093/acprof:oso/9780199751471.003.0006

Eisen, R. (2011b). Rabbinic Judaism. *Oxford University Press EBooks*, 65–110. https://doi.org/10.1093/acprof:oso/9780199751471.003.0003

Elia Levita. (2024, January 6). Wikipedia. https://en.wikipedia.org/wiki/Elia_Levita

Encyclopedia Britannica. (2019). Zionism | definition, history, examples, & facts. In *Encyclopædia Britannica*. https://www.britannica.com/topic/Zionism

Episode 2 – Aliyah Bet. (n.d.). The National WWII Museum New Orleans. https://www.nationalww2museum.org/war/podcasts/best-my-ability-podcast/season-2-archive/episode-2-aliyah-bet

Essene. (n.d.). Encyclopedia Britannica. https://www.britannica.com/topic/Essene

Essenes. (2024, January 29). Wikipedia. https://en.wikipedia.org/w/index.php?title=Essenes&oldid=1200326415

Essenes in Judaean society: The sectarians of the dead sea scrolls. (2021, January 17). OUPblog - Oxford University Press. https://blog.oup.com/2021/01/essenes-in-judaean-society-the-sectarians-of-the-dead-sea-scrolls/

Establishment of Israel. (2020). In *Encyclopædia Britannica*. https://www.britannica.com/place/Israel/Establishment-of-Israel

Esterson, G. L. (n.d.). *Renaissance (1300-1700)*. The given Names Data Bases (GNDBs).

https://www.jewishgen.org/databases/givennames/re
nasanc.htm
Eugenics and antisemitism – the holocaust explained: Designed for schools. (1933, January 30). The Holocaust Explained.
https://www.theholocaustexplained.org/how-and-why/why/eugenics-and-antisemitism/
Expulsions and exoduses of Jews. (2024, January 5). Wikipedia.
https://en.wikipedia.org/w/index.php?title=Expulsio
ns_and_exoduses_of_Jews&oldid=1193780973
Expulsions of Jews. (n.d.). Jewish Virtual Library.
https://www.jewishvirtuallibrary.org/expulsions
Ezra–Nehemiah. (2023, December 18). Wikipedia.
https://en.wikipedia.org/w/index.php?title=Ezra%E2
%80%93Nehemiah&oldid=1190572642
Ferguson, A. (n.d.). *Orthodox Judaism: Beliefs & concep.* Study.com.
https://study.com/academy/lesson/orthodox-judaism-beliefs-lesson-quiz.html
Fieldhouse, D. K. (2008). Palestine: The British mandate, 1918–1948. *Western Imperialism in the Middle East 1914-1958*, 151–219.
https://doi.org/10.1093/acprof:oso/9780199540839.003.0005
Figures in the history of Israel. (n.d.). The National Library of Israel.
https://www.nli.org.il/en/discover/israel/figures
Fisher, E. J. (1976). Cultic prostitution in the ancient near east? A reassessment. *Biblical Theology Bulletin: Journal of Bible and Culture*, 6(2-3), 225–236.
https://doi.org/10.1177/014610797600600306
"For the dead and the living, we must bear witness." – Elie Wiesel. (2019). the Jerusalem Post.
https://www.jpost.com/Blogs/Israel-Behind-the-Headlines/For-the-dead-and-the-living-we-must-bear-witness-Elie-Wiesel-488809
From citizens to outcasts, 1933–1938. (n.d.). United States Holocaust Museum.
https://www.ushmm.org/learn/holocaust/from-citizens-to-outcasts-1933-1938

Galicia. (n.d.). The Yivo Encyclopedia of Jews in Eastern Europe. https://yivoencyclopedia.org/article.aspx/galicia

Geller, J. (2022, January 3). *Digital media trends Jewish nonprofits should watch for in 2022.* EJewish Philanthropy. https://ejewishphilanthropy.com/digital-media-trends-jewish-nonprofits-should-watch-for-in-2022/

Geonim. (2023, September 17). Wikipedia. https://en.wikipedia.org/w/index.php?title=Geonim&oldid=1175744680

Ghert-Zand, R. (n.d.). Rethinking the "secret sauce" behind Jewish survival. *The TImes of Israel.* Retrieved February 30, 2013, from https://www.timesofisrael.com/rethinking-the-secret-sauce-behind-jewish-survival/

Ghettos In The holocaust. (2018). Imperial War Museums; Imperial War Museums. https://www.iwm.org.uk/history/ghettos-in-the-holocaust

Gidi Grinstein on the "secret sauce." (2024, January 10). The Jerusalem Post. https://www.jpost.com/diaspora/article-781553

Global: Social media companies must step up crisis response on Israel-Palestine as online hate and censorship proliferate. (2023, October 27). Amnesty International. https://www.amnesty.org/en/latest/news/2023/10/global-social-media-companies-must-step-up-crisis-response-on-israel-palestine-as-online-hate-and-censorship-proliferate/

Glossary. (2019). Jewish Virtual Library. https://www.jewishvirtuallibrary.org/glossary

Glossary of Jewish terminology. (n.d.). Judaism 101. https://www.jewfaq.org/glossary_of_jewish_terminology

Glossary of Jewish terms. (n.d.). Congregation Anshai Emeth. https://www.anshaiemeth.org/get-involved/welcome-judaism/glossary-jewish-terms/

Golden age of Jewish culture in Spain. (2024, January 14). Wikipedia.

https://en.wikipedia.org/w/index.php?title=Golden_a
ge_of_Jewish_culture_in_Spain&oldid=1195706341

Govier, G. (n.d.). *Biblical archaeology's top 10 discoveries
of 2020*. News & Reporting.
https://www.christianitytoday.com/news/2020/dece
mber/biblical-archaeology-new-discoveries-2020-
bible-artifacts.html

Greenberg, I. (n.d.). *The temple and its destruction*. My
Jewish Learning.
https://www.myjewishlearning.com/article/the-
temple-its-destruction/

Gucker, J. (n.d.). *Reform Judaism: Beliefs & history*.
Study.com.
https://study.com/academy/lesson/reform-judaism-
beliefs-history-quiz.html

Gucker, J. (2022). *Hasidic Judaism | definition, rules &
beliefs*. Study.com.
https://study.com/learn/lesson/hasidic-judaism-
rules-customs.html

Gunkel, H., & Hanson, K. C. (2009). Israel and Babylon:
The Babylonian influence on Israelite religion. In
JSTOR (1st ed.). The Lutterworth Press.
https://www.jstor.org/stable/j.ctt1cgf7gp

Haddad, M., & Chughtai, A. (2023, November 27). *A brief
history of Israel-Palestine conflict in 10 maps*. Al
Jazeera.
https://www.aljazeera.com/news/2023/11/27/palesti
ne-and-israel-brief-history-maps-and-charts

Hammerman, J., & Hammerman, S. (n.d.). *Jewish
history—to the middle ages*. Khan Academy.
https://www.khanacademy.org/humanities/ap-art-
history/introduction-cultures-religions-apah/judaism-
apah/a/jewish-historyto-the-middle-ages

Hasidic Judaism. (2024, February 5). Wikipedia.
https://en.wikipedia.org/w/index.php?title=Hasidic_
Judaism&oldid=1203522368

Hasidic movement: A history. (2003, September 11). My
Jewish Learning; My Jewish Learning.
https://www.myjewishlearning.com/article/hasidic-
movement-a-history/

Haskalah. (2024, February 1). Wikipedia. https://en.wikipedia.org/w/index.php?title=Haskalah &oldid=1201881287

Hasmonean dynasty. (n.d.). Encyclopaedia Britannica. Retrieved November 13, 2021, from https://www.britannica.com/topic/Hasmonean-dynasty

Hasmoneans. (n.d.). Encyclopedia.com. https://www.encyclopedia.com/people/philosophy-and-religion/judaism-biographies/hasmoneans

Hebrew language. (2019, March 18). Wikipedia. https://en.wikipedia.org/wiki/Hebrew_language

Hellenism. (n.d.). Jewish Virtual Library. https://www.jewishvirtuallibrary.org/hellenism-2

Hellenism & Judaism. (n.d.). My Jewish Learning. https://www.myjewishlearning.com/article/hellenism-judaism/

Hellenism and Judaism. (2013, October 4). Spiritual Discipleship. https://www.livestransforming.com/hellenism-and-judaism/

Hellenistic Judaism. (2024, January 18). Wikipedia. https://en.wikipedia.org/w/index.php?title=Hellenistic_Judaism&oldid=1196671998

Heschel, S. (2020, September 25). *Ending exile with the prophetic voice of the diasporic Jew*. Contending Modernities. https://contendingmodernities.nd.edu/theorizing-modernities/ending-exile/

Hess, R. (2023, May 26). *History of ancient Israelite religion*. https://www.oxfordbibliographies.com/display/document/obo-9780195393361/obo-9780195393361-0315.xml

Historical Jewish population. (2024, February 8). Wikipedia. https://en.wikipedia.org/w/index.php?title=Historical_Jewish_population&oldid=1204885484

History & overview of reform Judaism. (2013). Jewish Virtual Library.

https://www.jewishvirtuallibrary.org/history-and-overview-of-reform-judaism

History of ancient Israel and Judah. (2024, February 28). Wikipedia. https://en.wikipedia.org/w/index.php?title=History of ancient Israel and Judah&oldid=1210788991

History of european Jews in the middle ages. (2024, January 24). Wikipedia. https://en.wikipedia.org/w/index.php?title=History of European Jews in the Middle Ages&oldid=1198671885

History of Israel. (2024, February 4). Wikipedia. https://en.wikipedia.org/w/index.php?title=History of Israel&oldid=1203225373

History of Jewish immigration to Israel (Aliyah). (2012, December 14). ReformJudaism.org. https://reformjudaism.org/history-jewish-immigration-israel-aliyah

History of reform Judaism and a look ahead. (n.d.). Reform Judaism. https://reformjudaism.org/beliefs-practices/what-reform-judaism/history-reform-judaism-and-look-ahead-search-belonging

History of the Jews and the crusades. (2023, November 24). Wikipedia. https://en.wikipedia.org/w/index.php?title=History of the Jews and the Crusades&oldid=1186693982

History of the Jews in colonial America. (2024, February 6). Wikipedia. https://en.wikipedia.org/w/index.php?title=History of the Jews in Colonial America&oldid=1204048075

History of the Jews in iran. (2024, January 24). Wikipedia. https://en.wikipedia.org/w/index.php?title=History of the Jews in Iran&oldid=1198662864

The history of Jews in Latin America. (n.d.). Virtual Jewish Library. Retrieved March 2, 2024, from https://www.jewishvirtuallibrary.org/the-history-of-jews-in-latin-america

History of the Jews in the Byzantine empire. (2023, November 17). Wikipedia. https://en.wikipedia.org/w/index.php?title=History

of the Jews in the Byzantine Empire&oldid=1185
534381

History of the Jews in the Roman empire. (2019,
November 3). Wikipedia.
https://en.wikipedia.org/wiki/History_of_the_Jews
_in_the_Roman_Empire

History of the Jews in the United States. (2024, February
6). Wikipedia.
https://en.wikipedia.org/w/index.php?title=History
_of_the_Jews_in_the_United_States&oldid=1204047
894

History of the Jews under Muslim rule. (2024, January 21).
Wikipedia.
https://en.wikipedia.org/w/index.php?title=History
_of_the_Jews_under_Muslim_rule&oldid=119775993
6

History of Zionism: Revision history. (n.d.). Wikipedia.
Retrieved February 6, 2024, from
https://en.wikipedia.org/w/index.php?title=History
_of_Zionism&action=history

*How did the Jewish people understand and make sense of
the destruction of the Second Temple?* (n.d.). Mi
Yodeya. Retrieved February 5, 2024, from
https://judaism.stackexchange.com/questions/62096
/how-did-the-jewish-people-understand-and-make-
sense-of-the-destruction-of-the-se

*How the rabbis adapted Roman culture to create Judaism
as we know it.* (n.d.). The Bible and Interpretation
University of Arizona.
https://bibleinterp.arizona.edu/articles/2017/01/vis4
18018

*How to apply the Jewish intellectual tradition to achieve
success.* (n.d.). Touro University.
https://www.touro.edu/news--events/stories/how-to-
apply-the-jewish-intellectual-tradition-to-achieve-
success.php

Howard, B. (n.d.). *Research Guides: Judaism: Art &
architecture.* Southern Adventist University.
https://southern.libguides.com/judaism/art

Immigrants to Israel: 1948-1952. (n.d.). Jewish Virtual
Library.

https://www.jewishvirtuallibrary.org/immigrants-to-israel-1948-1952

In what ways did Jews contribute to medieval European economies? (2023). Tutor Chase. https://www.tutorchase.com/answers/ib/history/in-what-ways-did-jews-contribute-to-medieval-european-economies

Iranian impact on Judaism. (n.d.). University of Idaho. https://www.webpages.uidaho.edu/ngier/309/zorojud.htm

Iranian influence on Judaism. (n.d.). The Bible and Interpretation the University of Arizona. https://bibleinterp.arizona.edu/articles/sil358017

Islamic–Jewish relations. (2023, December 22). Wikipedia. https://en.wikipedia.org/w/index.php?title=Islamic%E2%80%93Jewish_relations&oldid=1191304140

Israel economic snapshot. (n.d.). OECD. https://www.oecd.org/economy/israel-economic-snapshot/

Israel - Immigration and conflict. (2020). In *Encyclopædia Britannica.* https://www.britannica.com/place/Israel/Immigration-and-conflict

Israel, J. (2017, April 21). *How did the enlightenment shape the Jews?* UW Stroum Center for Jewish Studies. https://jewishstudies.washington.edu/jewish-history-and-thought/did-enlightenment-shape-jews-jonathan-israel/

Israel's moment of crisis: What are the prospects for political change? (n.d.). Middle East Institute. Retrieved February 6, 2024, from https://www.mei.edu/events/israels-moment-crisis-what-are-prospects-political-change

Israeli–Palestinian conflict. (2024, February 6). Wikipedia. https://en.wikipedia.org/w/index.php?title=Israeli%E2%80%93Palestinian_conflict&oldid=1204279418

Israelite highland settlement. (2023, December 16). Wikipedia. https://en.wikipedia.org/w/index.php?title=Israelite_highland_settlement&oldid=1190189935

Israelites. (2024, February 1). Wikipedia.
https://en.wikipedia.org/w/index.php?title=Israelites
&oldid=1202058546

Israelites found in Egypt. (n.d.). The BAS Library.
Retrieved January 19, 2024, from
https://library.biblicalarchaeology.org/article/israelite
s-found-in-egypt/

Jacobs, J. (n.d.). *Maimonides.* Internet Encyclopedia of
Philosophy. https://iep.utm.edu/maimonid/

Jaspal, R., & Yampolsky, M. A. (2011). Social
representations of the Holocaust and Jewish Israeli
identity construction: insights from identity process
theory. *Social Identities, 17*(2), 201–224.
https://doi.org/10.1080/13504630.2011.558374

Jewish Americans in 2020. (2021, May 11). Pew Research
Center's Religion & Public Life Project.
https://www.pewresearch.org/religion/2021/05/11/je
wish-americans-in-2020/

*Jewish Americans share views on conflict as Israel-Hamas
war continues.* (2023, November 14). PBS.
https://www.pbs.org/newshour/show/jewish-
americans-share-views-on-conflict-as-israel-hamas-
war-continues

Jewish assimilation. (2024, January 22). Wikipedia.
https://en.wikipedia.org/w/index.php?title=Jewish_a
ssimilation&oldid=1197826134

Jewish diaspora. (2024, February 3). Wikipedia.
https://en.wikipedia.org/w/index.php?title=Jewish_d
iaspora&oldid=1202583346

Jewish emancipation. (2024, January 14). Wikipedia.
https://en.wikipedia.org/w/index.php?title=Jewish_e
mancipation&oldid=1195675014

Jewish heritage: The golden age. (2019, April 17). Jewish
Heritage Alliance.
https://jewishheritagealliance.com/jewish-heritage-
the-golden-age/

Jewish migration histories - politics. (n.d.). The National
Archives. Retrieved February 6, 2024, from
https://webarchive.nationalarchives.gov.uk/+/http:/w
ww.movinghere.org.uk/galleries/histories/jewish/poli
tics/politics.htm

Jewish philosophy. (2024, January 13). Wikipedia.
https://en.wikipedia.org/w/index.php?title=Jewish_p
hilosophy&oldid=1195299464

Jewish population of the world. (2023). Jewish Virtual
Library. https://www.jewishvirtuallibrary.org/jewish-
population-of-the-world#large

Jewish resistance. (2014). United States Holocaust
Memorial Museum.
https://encyclopedia.ushmm.org/content/en/article/j
ewish-resistance

Jewish resistance to the holocaust. (2021). The Wiener
Holocaust Library.
https://wienerholocaustlibrary.org/exhibition/jewish-
resistance-to-the-holocaust/

Jewish–Roman wars. (2023, December 4). Wikipedia.
https://en.wikipedia.org/w/index.php?title=Jewish%
E2%80%93Roman_wars&oldid=1188230679

Jews in early America - Touro synagogue. (2022, January
20). Touro Synagogue.
https://tourosynagogue.org/history/jews-in-early-
america/

Joellyn Zollman. (2002, August 18). *Jewish immigration to
America: Three waves*. My Jewish Learning; My
Jewish Learning.
https://www.myjewishlearning.com/article/jewish-
immigration-to-america-three-waves/

Judaea (Roman province). (2024, January 31). Wikipedia.
https://en.wikipedia.org/w/index.php?title=Judaea_(
Roman_province)&oldid=1201544000

Judah during Persian Rule. (n.d.). Enter the Bible.
https://enterthebible.org/time-period/judah-during-
persian-rule

Judaism after the temple. (n.d.). My Jewish Learning.
https://www.myjewishlearning.com/article/judaism-
after-the-temple/

Judaism and Christianity and the dead sea scrolls. (2010,
July 27). Library of Congress.
https://www.loc.gov/exhibits/scrolls/juda.html

*Judaism and the Hellenistic experience: A classical model
for living in two cultures*. (1956, August 1).
Commentary Magazine.

https://www.commentary.org/articles/moses-
hadas/judaism-and-the-hellenistic-experience-a-
classical-model-for-living-in-two-cultures/
Judaism at the speed of technological change. (n.d.).
SAPIR Journal.
https://sapirjournal.org/technology/2023/12/judaism
-at-the-speed-of-technological-change/
Judaism develops. (2017). Khan Academy.
https://www.khanacademy.org/humanities/world-
history/ancient-medieval/judaism/a/judaism-
develops
Judaism glossary terms. (n.d.). The Pluralism Project:
Harvard University. https://pluralism.org/judaism-
glossary-terms
*Judaism: A supplemental resource for grade 12 world of
religions: A canadian perspective diversity of judaism
diversity of religious interpretation and practice.*
(n.d.).
https://www.edu.gov.mb.ca/k12/docs/support/world
religions/judaism/diversity.pdf
Judea under Byzantine rule. (n.d.). Jewish Virtual Library.
Retrieved February 5, 2024, from
https://www.jewishvirtuallibrary.org/judea-under-
byzantine-rule
Kant, I. (n.d.). *An Answer to the Question: What is
Enlightenment? (1784).* Jim Donelan's Course Page:
UCSB.
https://donelan.faculty.writing.ucsb.edu/enlight.html
Kaplan, J. (2002, December 24). *The mass migration to
Israel of the 1950s.* My Jewish Learning; My Jewish
Learning.
https://www.myjewishlearning.com/article/the-mass-
migration-of-the-1950s/
Kim, V. (2024, February 29). *Death toll in Gaza passes
30,000.* New York Times.
https://www.nytimes.com/2024/02/29/world/middle
east/gaza-death-toll-war.html
Klein, C. (2018, September). *How South America became a
Nazi haven.* History Channel.
https://www.history.com/news/how-south-america-
became-a-nazi-haven

Kopelwitz, I. K. (2023, October 21). *The war has forced Israel's Arab citizens to explain that no, they are not Hamas.* CNN. https://www.cnn.com/2023/10/21/middleeast/arab-israeli-citizens-cmd-intl/index.html

Krebs, J. (2024, January 10). *Gidi Grinstein on the "Secret Sauce."* The Jerusalem Post. https://www.jpost.com/diaspora/article-781553

Laura. (n.d.). *Zionism.* https://lsa.umich.edu/content/dam/cmenas-assets/cmenas-documents/unit-of-israel-palestine/Section1_Zionism.pdf

Lax, C. (2022, July 11). *New archaeological discoveries confirm ancient connection of Israel to the Jewish people.* The Algemeiner. https://www.algemeiner.com/2022/07/11/new-archaeological-discoveries-confirm-ancient-connection-of-israel-to-the-jewish-people/

Levant. (2024, January 17). Wikipedia. https://en.wikipedia.org/w/index.php?title=Levant&oldid=1196511812

Levant meaning & facts. (n.d.). Encyclopedia Britannica. https://www.britannica.com/place/Levant

Life in the ghettos. (2019). United States Holocaust Memorial Museum. https://encyclopedia.ushmm.org/content/en/article/life-in-the-ghettos

Linfield, H. S. (1919). The relation of jewish to babylonian law. *The American Journal of Semitic Languages and Literatures, 36*(1), 40–66. https://www.jstor.org/stable/528222

Lipman, D. (2019, September 26). *Operation Moses: The rescue of Ethiopian Jews.* HonestReporting. https://honestreporting.com/operation-moses-the-rescue-of-ethiopian-jews/

List of Zionists. (2023, December 9). Wikipedia. https://en.wikipedia.org/w/index.php?title=List_of_Zionists&oldid=1189070191

Liu, J. (2013, October 1). *A portrait of Jewish Americans.* Pew Research Center's Religion & Public Life Project.

https://www.pewresearch.org/religion/2013/10/01/je
wish-american-beliefs-attitudes-culture-survey/
Living conditions. (n.d.). Państwowe Muzeum Na
Majdanku.
https://www.majdanek.eu/en/history/living_conditio
ns/13
Lohnes, K. (2019). Siege of Jerusalem. In *Encyclopædia
Britannica.* https://www.britannica.com/event/Siege-
of-Jerusalem-70
Ludlow, J. W. (n.d.). *Destruction of the second temple in 70
CE.* BYU Religious Studies Center.
https://rpl.hds.harvard.edu/faq/destruction-second-
temple-70-ce
Ludlow, J. W. (2019). *The first Jewish revolt against
Rome.* Byu Religious Studies Center.
https://rsc.byu.edu/new-testament-history-culture-
society/first-jewish-revolt-against-rome
Maccabean revolt. (2024, January 23). Wikipedia.
https://en.wikipedia.org/w/index.php?title=Maccabea
n_Revolt&oldid=1198104172
Maccabean revolt facts for kids. (n.d.). Kids Encyclopedia
Facts. Retrieved February 5, 2024, from
https://kids.kiddle.co/Maccabean_Revolt
Maccabees. (n.d.). Encyclopedia Britannica. Retrieved
February 9, 2021, from
https://www.britannica.com/topic/Maccabees
Magee, M. D. (2024). *How Persia created Judaism:
Persian and Jewish religion.* Katehon.
https://katehon.com/en/article/how-persia-created-
judaism-persian-and-jewish-religion
Mandate for Palestine. (2024, February 1). Wikipedia.
https://en.wikipedia.org/w/index.php?title=Mandate
_for_Palestine&oldid=1201804089
Maor, M. (2009). *Israel studies an anthology: The history
of Zionism.* Jewish Virtual Library.
https://www.jewishvirtuallibrary.org/israel-studies-
an-anthology-the-history-of-zionism
*Mark R. Cohen The "Golden Age" of Jewish-Muslim
Relations: Myth and reality.* (n.d.).
https://assets.press.princeton.edu/chapters/p10098.p
df

Marx, D. (2013). the missing temple: The status of the temple in Jewish culture following its destruction. *European Judaism: A Journal for the New Europe*, *46*(2), 61–78. https://www.jstor.org/stable/42751139

Marx, E., Hertzog, E., Goldberg, H., & Abuhav, O. (Eds.). (2009, November). *Perspectives on Israeli anthropology*. Wayne State University Press. https://www.wsupress.wayne.edu/books/detail/persp ectives-israeli-anthropology

Medicine. (2013). Jewish Virtual Library. https://www.jewishvirtuallibrary.org/medicine

Medieval European Judaism (950–1750). (n.d.). Encyclopedia Britannica. Retrieved September 1, 2020, from https://www.britannica.com/topic/Judaism/Medieval -European-Judaism-950-1750

Medieval Muslim societies. (2017). Khan Academy. https://www.khanacademy.org/humanities/world-history/medieval-times/social-institutions-in-the-islamic-world/a/medieval-muslim-societies

Meier, D. A. (n.d.). *Review of The Founding fathers of Zionism by Benzion Netanyahu*. ASMEA: Association for the Study of the Middle East and Africa. Retrieved February 6, 2024, from https://www.asmeascholars.org/the-founding-fathers-of-zionism

Merneptah Stele. (2020, October 28). Wikipedia. https://en.wikipedia.org/wiki/Merneptah_Stele

Milestones: 1945–1952. (2019). Office of the Historian. https://history.state.gov/milestones/1945-1952/creation-israel

Milestones: 1961–1968. (2019). Office of the Historian. https://history.state.gov/milestones/1961-1968/arab-israeli-war-1967

Mishnah. (n.d.). Sefaria. https://www.sefaria.org/texts/Mishnah

Mishnah. (2024, January 20). Wikipedia. https://en.wikipedia.org/w/index.php?title=Mishnah &oldid=1197433894

Mosaic religion. (2019). In *Encyclopædia Britannica*.
https://www.britannica.com/topic/Judaism/Mosaic-religion

Mullen, P. B. W. (2015, October 21). *Israeli Palestinian conflict: Two viewpoints; one tragic outcome*. CNN.
https://edition.cnn.com/2015/10/21/middleeast/israeli-palestinian-root-of-violence/index.html

Nadler, S. (2003). Review of Judaism and Enlightenment by Adam Sutcliffe. *Notre Dame Philosophical Reviews*. https://ndpr.nd.edu/reviews/judaism-and-enlightenment/

Nappa, M. (2019, May 15). *Who were the sadducees in the Bible? What were their beliefs?* Christianity.com.
https://www.christianity.com/wiki/people/who-were-the-sadducees-in-the-bible-what-were-their-beliefs.html

Nazi Germany. (2024, February 1). Wikipedia.
https://en.wikipedia.org/w/index.php?title=Nazi_Germany&oldid=1201950467

Nelson, R. (2020, April 21). *Who were the Pharisees? The beginner's guide*. OverviewBible.
https://overviewbible.com/pharisees/

New survey of US Jews reveals worries, strengths, divisions. (2021, May 11). AP NEWS.
https://apnews.com/article/donald-trump-middle-east-race-and-ethnicity-religion-811fb850be613d16eec24949596603a9

1948 Arab–Israeli War. (2024, February 1). Wikipedia.
https://en.wikipedia.org/w/index.php?title=1948_Arab%E2%80%93Israeli_War&oldid=1201696376

1948 Palestine war. (2024, February 28). Wikipedia.
https://en.wikipedia.org/w/index.php?title=1948_Palestine_war&oldid=1210785911

1990s post-Soviet aliyah. (2024, January 18). Wikipedia.
https://en.wikipedia.org/w/index.php?title=1990s_post-Soviet_aliyah&oldid=1196772321

Oates, H. (2015, October 29). *The Maccabean revolt*. World History Encyclopedia.
https://www.worldhistory.org/article/827/the-maccabean-revolt/

Old City. (2013, July 16). Emek Shave.
https://emekshaveh.org/en/old-city/
Operation Solomon. (n.d.). JDC. https://www.jdc.org/operation-solomon/
Origins of Judaism. (2024, February 4). Wikipedia.
https://en.wikipedia.org/w/index.php?title=Origins_of_Judaism&oldid=1203083776
Orthodox Judaism. (2024, February 5). Wikipedia.
https://en.wikipedia.org/w/index.php?title=Orthodox_Judaism&oldid=1203886105
Pale of Settlement. (n.d.). The Yivo Encyclopedia of Jews in Eastern Europe.
https://yivoencyclopedia.org/article.aspx/pale_of_settlement
Palmer, J. (2021, February 10). *The Jewish intellectual tradition.* Jewish Standard.
https://jewishstandard.timesofisrael.com/the-jewish-intellectual-tradition/
Patton, C. (2017, March). *What made Nehemiah an effective leader?* The Journal of Applied Christian Leadership. https://jacl.andrews.edu/what-made-nehemiah-an-effective-leader/
Perez, R. (n.d.). *History in the making history in the making Palestinian-jews and Israel's dual identity crisis.*
https://scholarworks.lib.csusb.edu/cgi/viewcontent.cgi?article=1052&context=history-in-the-making
Persia. (n.d.). Jewish Virtual Library.
https://www.jewishvirtuallibrary.org/persia
Persian and Hellenistic influences. (n.d.). Encyclopaedia Britannica.
https://www.britannica.com/topic/biblical-literature/Persian-and-Hellenistic-influences
Persian rule (539 – 331 B.C.). (n.d.). Bible Study. Retrieved February 5, 2024, from
http://mybiblicalstudy.weebly.com/persian-rule-539-ndash-331-bc.html
Pharisees. (2024, January 30). Wikipedia.
https://en.wikipedia.org/w/index.php?title=Pharisees&oldid=1201081562

Philistines. (2020, January 9). Wikipedia.
https://en.wikipedia.org/wiki/Philistines
Picheta, R. (2024, February 29). *Gaza death toll: More than 30,000 killed since Israel-Hamas war began, health ministry says.* CNN.
https://www.cnn.com/2024/02/29/middleeast/gaza-death-toll-30000-israel-war-hnk-intl/index.html
Politics of Israel. (2023, October 19). Wikipedia.
https://en.wikipedia.org/w/index.php?title=Politics_of_Israel&oldid=1180911056
Posner, M. (n.d.). *What Is Rabbinic Judaism?* Chabad.
https://www.chabad.org/library/article_cdo/aid/6031379/jewish/What-Is-Rabbinic-Judaism.htm
Protestantism in Germany. (2023, September 14). Wikipedia.
https://en.wikipedia.org/w/index.php?title=Protestantism_in_Germany&oldid=1175325434
Quandt, W. B. (1995, November). *The Zionist ideology.* Foreign Affairs; University Press Of New England.
https://www.foreignaffairs.com/reviews/capsule-review/1995-11-01/zionist-ideology
Rabbinic Judaism. (2019). In *Encyclopædia Britannica.*
https://www.britannica.com/topic/Rabbinic-Judaism
Rabbinic Judaism. (2024, January 31). Wikipedia.
https://en.wikipedia.org/w/index.php?title=Rabbinic_Judaism&oldid=1201328681
Ram, U. (1995). Zionist historiography and the invention of modern Jewish nationhood: The case of Ben Zion Dinur. *History and Memory, 7*(1), 91–124.
https://www.jstor.org/stable/25618681
Raphael, M. (2016). Judaism and visual art. *Oxford Research Encyclopedia of Religion.*
https://doi.org/10.1093/acrefore/9780199340378.013.98
Razin, A. (2017, March). *NBER Working Paper Series: Working Paper 23210: Israel's immigration story: Globalization lessons.* National Bureau of Economic Research.
Refael, T. (2018, August 10). *Continuity, Persian style.* Jewish Journal.

https://jewishjournal.com/commentary/columnist/23
7116/continuity-persian-style/

Reform Judaism. (2024, February 2). Wikipedia.
https://en.wikipedia.org/w/index.php?title=Reform
Judaism&oldid=1202352158

Reformation. (n.d.). Jewish Virtual Library.
https://www.jewishvirtuallibrary.org/reformation

Religion Library: Orthodox Judaism. (n.d.). Patheos.
https://www.patheos.com/library/orthodox-judaism

Rendsburg, G. A. (n.d.). *The emergence of israel in the land
of canaan.*
https://jewishstudies.rutgers.edu/docman/rendsburg
/877-ch-3-text-notes/file

Resistance during the holocaust. (2012). In *Anti-
Defamation League.*
https://www.adl.org/sites/default/files/documents/as
sets/pdf/education-outreach/Resistance-During-the-
Holocaust-NYLM-Guide.pdf

Return to Zion. (2024, February 5). Wikipedia.
https://en.wikipedia.org/w/index.php?title=Return_t
o_Zion&oldid=1203674039

Richard, S. (2008, January 1). *Archaeology of the near
east: The Levant* (D. M. Pearsall, Ed.). ScienceDirect;
Academic Press.
https://www.sciencedirect.com/science/article/abs/pi
i/B9780123739629003757

*Risk of Israeli-Palestinian conflict threatening stability of
wider region remains high, senior UN political
official warns security council.* (2023, December 29).
Reliefweb. https://reliefweb.int/report/occupied-
palestinian-territory/risk-israeli-palestinian-conflict-
threatening-stability-wider-region-remains-high-
senior-un-political-official-warns-security-council

*Role and contribution of Jews in medieval Europe (1095–
1492).* (2024). Tutor Chase.
https://www.tutorchase.com/notes/ib/history/21-2-
4-role-and-contribution-of-jews-in-medieval-europe-
1095-1492

Roman ghetto. (2024, February 18). Wikipedia.
https://en.wikipedia.org/w/index.php?title=Roman_
Ghetto&oldid=1208649299

Rutgers, L. (2017). *Roman policy towards the Jews.*
Printed Matter: Centro Primo Levi Online Monthly.
https://primolevicenter.org/printed-matter/roman-
policy-towards-the-jews-expulsions-from-the-city-of-
rome-during-the-first-century-c-e/

Sadducee. (n.d.). Encyclopedia Britannica. Retrieved March
6, 2020, from
https://www.britannica.com/topic/Sadducee

Sadducees. (2024, January 19). Wikipedia.
https://en.wikipedia.org/w/index.php?title=Sadducee
s&oldid=1197203601

Salzberg, A. (n.d.). *Judaism after the temple.* My Jewish
Learning.
https://www.myjewishlearning.com/article/judaism-
after-the-temple/

Sanitary conditions. (n.d.). Auschwitz.
https://auschwitz.net/auschwitz-sanitary-conditions/

Sarna, J. D., & Golden, J. (n.d.). *The American Jewish
experience in the twentieth century: Antisemitism and
assimilation.* National Humanities Center.
https://nationalhumanitiescenter.org/tserve/twenty/t
keyinfo/jewishexp.htm

Satmar Hasidism: History, community, and traditions.
(n.d.). Roundabout Theatre Company.
https://www.roundabouttheatre.org/get-
tickets/upstage-guides-current/the-wanderers-
upstage-guide/satmar-hasidism-history-community-
and-traditions/

Scheer, S. (2023, November 23). Israel's economic growth
to slow to 2% in 2023 due to war -finance ministry.
Reuters. https://www.reuters.com/world/middle-
east/israels-economic-growth-slow-2-2023-16-2024-
due-war-finance-ministry-2023-11-23/

Schiffman, L. H. (n.d.). *Palestine Under Persian Rule.* My
Jewish Learning.
https://www.myjewishlearning.com/article/palestine-
under-persian-rule/

Schiffman, L. H. (2003, July 16). *Building the second
temple.* My Jewish Learning.
https://www.myjewishlearning.com/article/second-
temple/

Schoenberg, S. (n.d.). *The Haskalah*. Jewish Virtual
    Library. https://www.jewishvirtuallibrary.org/the-
    haskalah
Schumacher-Brunhes, M. (n.d.). *Enlightenment Jewish
    Style: The Haskalah movement in Europe*. EGO:
    European History Online. http://ieg-
    ego.eu/en/threads/european-networks/jewish-
    networks/marie-schumacher-brunhes-enlightenment-
    jewish-style-the-haskalah-movement-in-europe
Sea peoples. (2019, October 13). Wikipedia.
    https://en.wikipedia.org/wiki/Sea_Peoples
Second aliyah. (2024, February 18). Wikipedia.
    https://en.wikipedia.org/w/index.php?title=Second_
    Aliyah&oldid=1208696334
Second temple. (2024, January 15). Wikipedia.
    https://en.wikipedia.org/w/index.php?title=Second_
    Temple&oldid=1195933448
Second Temple period. (2023, December 11). Wikipedia.
    https://en.wikipedia.org/w/index.php?title=Second_
    Temple_period&oldid=1189415494
Seeking justice. (n.d.). Holocaust Memorial Day Trust.
    https://www.hmd.org.uk/learn-about-the-holocaust-
    and-genocides/the-holocaust/seeking-justice/
Seidelman, R. D. (2012). Conflicts of quarantine: The case
    of Jewish immigrants to the Jewish state. *American
    Journal of Public Health, 102*(2), 243–252.
    https://doi.org/10.2105/ajph.2011.300476
*70 years after WWII, the holocaust is still very important
    to American Jews*. (2015, August 13). Pew Research
    Center. https://www.pewresearch.org/short-
    reads/2015/08/13/70-years-after-wwii-the-holocaust-
    is-still-very-important-to-american-jews/
Shepherds' crusade (1320). (2024, March 3). Wikipedia.
    https://en.wikipedia.org/w/index.php?title=Shepherd
    s%27_Crusade_(1320)&oldid=1211669524
Siege of Jerusalem (70 CE). (2023, December 19).
    Wikipedia.
    https://en.wikipedia.org/w/index.php?title=Siege_of
    Jerusalem(70_CE)&oldid=1190796543

Siege of Jerusalem (587 BC). (2024, January 3). Wikipedia.
https://en.wikipedia.org/w/index.php?title=Siege_of_Jerusalem_(587_BC)&oldid=1193286596

Six facts about threats to the Jewish community. (2022, January 16). ADL.
https://www.adl.org/resources/blog/six-facts-about-threats-jewish-community

Smith, J. (2023, October 31). *Analysis: A new wave of antisemitism threatens to rock an already unstable world*. CNN.
https://www.cnn.com/2023/10/31/politics/antisemitism-unstable-world-analysis/index.html

Solomon. (2024, February 1). Wikipedia.
https://en.wikipedia.org/w/index.php?title=Solomon&oldid=1201971885

Sources and parallels of the Exodus. (2024, January 31). Wikipedia.
https://en.wikipedia.org/w/index.php?title=Sources_and_parallels_of_the_Exodus&oldid=1201433198

Spiro, K. (2023, March 5). *These seven 19th century Jewish inventors changed your life*. Aish.
https://aish.com/these-seven-19th-century-jewish-inventors-changed-your-life/

Spitzer, J. (n.d.). *After the first temple*. My Jewish Learning.
https://www.myjewishlearning.com/article/after-the-first-temple/

Spokoiny, A. (2023, July 26). *The second temple's destruction serves as a warning for today*. EJewish Philanthropy. https://ejewishphilanthropy.com/the-second-temples-destruction-serves-as-a-warning-for-today/

Stein, K. (2020, May 15). *The Arab-Israeli War of 1948—A short history*. CIE: Center of Israel Education.
https://israeled.org/the-arab-israeli-war-of-1948-a-short-history/

Tahhan, Z. (2018, November 2). *More than a century on: The Balfour declaration explained*. AlJazeera; Aljazeera.
https://www.aljazeera.com/features/2018/11/2/more-than-a-century-on-the-balfour-declaration-explained

Talmud. (2024, January 27). Wikipedia.
https://en.wikipedia.org/w/index.php?title=Talmud&
oldid=1199754982

Talmudic academies in Babylonia. (2023, September 11).
Wikipedia.
https://en.wikipedia.org/w/index.php?title=Talmudic
_academies_in_Babylonia&oldid=1174946327

*10 ways to have conscientious conversations on the
Israeli-Palestinian conflict.* (n.d.). Anti-Defamation
League. https://www.adl.org/resources/tools-and-
strategies/10-ways-have-conscientious-conversations-
israeli-palestinian

The "Persian" period. (n.d.). Oxford Bibliographies.
https://www.oxfordbibliographies.com/display/docu
ment/obo-9780195393361/obo-9780195393361-
0194.xml

The age of the patriarchs. (2019). Jewish Virtual Library.
https://www.jewishvirtuallibrary.org/the-age-of-the-
patriarchs

The Arab spring and mideast peace. (2011, November 8).
United States Institute of Peace.
https://www.usip.org/publications/2011/11/arab-
spring-and-mideast-peace

The Arab-Israeli war of 1948. (n.d.). Office of the
Historian. https://history.state.gov/milestones/1945-
1952/arab-israeli-war

The Babylonbian exile and the Jewish religion. (n.d.).
Jewish Wikipedia.
http://www.jewishwikipedia.info/movement_babylon
.html

The Babylonian exile. (n.d.). Encyclopedia Britannica.
Retrieved April 22, 2021, from
https://www.britannica.com/topic/Judaism/The-
Babylonian-Exile

The Babylonian exile. (2019). Jewish Virtual Library.
https://www.jewishvirtuallibrary.org/the-babylonian-
exile

The British Museum. (n.d.). *Canaanites, an introduction.*
Khan Academy.
https://www.khanacademy.org/humanities/ancient-
art-civilizations/ancient-near-

east1/x7e914f5b:canaanites/a/canaanites-an-introduction
The challenge of assimilation. (n.d.). Pluralism.
https://pluralism.org/the-challenge-of-assimilation
The core values of conservative Judaism. (2019). Jewish
Virtual Library.
https://www.jewishvirtuallibrary.org/the-core-values-of-conservative-judaism
The crusades. (2019). Jewish Virtual Library.
https://www.jewishvirtuallibrary.org/the-crusades
The destruction of the first holy temple. (n.d.). Chabad.
https://www.chabad.org/library/article_cdo/aid/1445
69/jewish/The-First-Temple.htm
The Diaspora. (n.d.). Jewish Virtual Library.org.
https://www.jewishvirtuallibrary.org/the-diaspora#google_vignette
The Editors of Encyclopaedia Britannica. (2019a). First
Jewish Revolt | 66-70 CE. In *Encyclopædia
Britannica.* https://www.britannica.com/event/First-Jewish-Revolt
The Editors of Encyclopaedia Britannica. (2019b). Reform
Judaism. In *Encyclopædia Britannica.*
https://www.britannica.com/topic/Reform-Judaism
The Editors of Encyclopedia Britannica. (2014a). Pharisee |
Jewish history. In *Encyclopædia Britannica.*
https://www.britannica.com/topic/Pharisee
The Editors of Encyclopedia Britannica. (2014b). Temple of
Jerusalem. In *Encyclopædia Britannica.*
https://www.britannica.com/topic/Temple-of-Jerusalem
The Editors of Encyclopedia Britannica. (2019). Babylonian
captivity. In *Encyclopædia Britannica.*
https://www.britannica.com/event/Babylonian-Captivity
The Hasmonean dynasty. (n.d.-a). Jewish Virtual Library.
https://www.jewishvirtuallibrary.org/the-hasmonean-dynasty
The Hasmonean dynasty. (n.d.-b). My Jewish Learning.
https://www.myjewishlearning.com/article/the-hasmonean-dynasty/

The Hasmoneans. (2010, February 22). JewishHistory.org.
https://www.jewishhistory.org/the-hasmoneans/

The Institute of Jewish Studies of the Jagiellonian
University in Krakow, The Institute of Middle and Far
East of the Jagiellonian University in Krakow , & The
European Association of Israel Studies a. (2018).
Social and Political Dynamics in Israel. Jewish State
70 Years after the Declaration of Independence. In
*https://orient.uj.edu.pl/documents/20745011/0/Soci
al+and+Political+Dynamics+in+Israel%2C+Krakow
+%281%29.pdf/2a90894c-40cb-4627-80a3-
bb9706df9d34.*

The Jewish Americans. (2019). PBS.
https://www.pbs.org/jewishamericans/jewish_life/as
similation.html

*The Jewish star: History, spirituality, and personal
resilience.* (2024, January 29). Alef Bet by Paula.
https://www.alefbet.com/blogs/blog/the-jewish-star-
a-fusion-of-history-spirituality-and-personal-
resilience

The Jews and the Renaissance. (2012). JewishHistory.org.
https://www.jewishhistory.org/the-jews-and-the-
renaissance/

The most important Zionist figures you need to know.
(2023, December 22). Judaica Webstore.
https://blog.judaicawebstore.com/zionist-figures/

The Nakba did not start or end in 1948. (2017, May 23).
AlJazeera.
https://www.aljazeera.com/features/2017/5/23/the-
nakba-did-not-start-or-end-in-1948

The Nazi rise to power. (2000). United States Holocaust
Memorial Museum; United States Holocaust Memorial
Museum.
https://encyclopedia.ushmm.org/content/en/article/t
he-nazi-rise-to-power

The Nuremberg trials. (n.d.). The National WWII Museum
New Orleans.
https://www.nationalww2museum.org/war/topics/nu
remberg-trials

The oral law - Talmud & Mishna. (2019). Jewish Virtual Library. https://www.jewishvirtuallibrary.org/the-oral-law-talmud-and-mishna

The Origins of Hasidism. (n.d.). PBS. https://www.pbs.org/alifeapart/intro_6.html

The Persian empire, the return of the Jews, and the diaspora. (2020). Church of Jesus Christ. https://www.churchofjesuschrist.org/study/manual/old-testament-student-manual-kings-malachi/enrichment-j?lang=eng

The Persians. (n.d.). Jewish Virtual Library. https://www.jewishvirtuallibrary.org/the-persians

The Roman empire: In the first century: Josephus & Judea. (2006). PBS. https://www.pbs.org/empires/romans/empire/josephus.html

The Roman empire: Jews in roman times. (2019). PBS. https://www.pbs.org/empires/romans/empire/jews.html

The second temple. (n.d.). Bible Odyssey. https://www.bibleodyssey.org/articles/the-second-temple/

The Talmud. (n.d.). Reform Judaism. https://www.reformjudaism.org/talmud

The Temple and its destruction. (n.d.). My Jewish Learning. https://www.myjewishlearning.com/article/the-temple-its-destruction/

The treatment of Jews in Arab/Islamic Countries. (n.d.). Jewish Virtual Library. https://www.jewishvirtuallibrary.org/the-treatment-of-jews-in-arab-islamic-countries

The Wiener Holocaust Library. (n.d.). *The early years of the Nazi Party – The Holocaust explained: Designed for schools.* The Holocaust Explained. https://www.theholocaustexplained.org/the-nazi-rise-to-power/the-early-years-of-the-nazi-party/

The world is broken, so humans must repair it: The history and evolution of tikkun olam. (n.d.). Brandeis University. https://www.brandeis.edu/jewish-experience/history-culture/2023/may/tikkun-olam-history.html

Timeline: Key events in the Israel-Arab and Israeli-Palestinian conflict. (2023, November 1). American Jewish Committee. https://www.ajc.org/IsraelConflictTimeline

Tzvi. (2020, December 24). *What is the Mishnah?* Aish. https://aish.com/the-mishnah-writing-down-jewish-law/

UN expert warns of new instance of mass ethnic cleansing of Palestinians, calls for immediate ceasefire. (2023, Summer). United Nations. https://www.ohchr.org/en/press-releases/2023/10/un-expert-warns-new-instance-mass-ethnic-cleansing-palestinians-calls

United States Holocaust Memorial Museum, Washington, DC. (2019). *Antisemitism in History: The era of Nationalism, 1800–1918.* United States Holocaust Memorial Museum. https://encyclopedia.ushmm.org/content/en/article/antisemitism-in-history-the-era-of-nationalism-1800-1918

von Mering, S. (2022, May 13). *How social media fuels antisemitism.* Brandeis University. https://www.brandeis.edu/jewish-experience/social-justice/2022/may/antisemitism-social-media.html

Wachsmann, N. (2000). *Daily life.* The Nazi Concentration Camps: A Teaching and Learning Resource. http://www.camps.bbk.ac.uk/themes/daily-life.html

Wachtel, D. (2013, April 3). *The Jews in the Italian Renaissance.* Sothebys; Sotheby's. https://www.sothebys.com/en/articles/the-jews-in-the-italian-renaissance

Weaver, H. R. (1949). The priesthood of Judaism in the Persian period. *Open.bu.edu.* https://open.bu.edu/handle/2144/6350

Wertheimer, J. (2022, January 16). *The challenges facing the American Jewish community.* Aish. https://aish.com/the-challenges-facing-the-american-jewish-community/

What effects did the babylonian exile have on the Jewish religion? (2013). Synonym.com.
https://classroom.synonym.com/effects-did-babylonian-exile-jewish-religion-7222.html

What is BDS? – boycott, divestment and sanctions. (n.d.). Jewish Voice for Peace.
https://www.jewishvoiceforpeace.org/resource/zionism/

What Is the Mishnah? (n.d.). My Jewish Learning.
https://www.myjewishlearning.com/article/mishnah/

What was the Babylonian captivity/exile? (2011, March 24). Got Questions.
https://www.gotquestions.org/Babylonian-captivity-exile.html

What's the most pressing issue facing American Jews? Answers from a new generation of Jewish leaders. (n.d.). Brandeis University.
https://www.brandeis.edu/jewish-experience/alumni-friends/2022/september/alumni-roundtable-judaism.html

Where did the early Israelites come from? (n.d.). The BAS Library. Retrieved February 5, 2024, from
https://library.biblicalarchaeology.org/collections/where-did-early-israelites-come/

Why the Jews: History of antisemitism. (2019). United States Holocaust Memorial Museum; United States Holocaust Memorial Museum.
https://www.ushmm.org/antisemitism/what-is-antisemitism/why-the-jews-history-of-antisemitism

Woodley, T. (2013, November). *Jewish immigration to historical Palestine.* CJPME - English.
https://www.cjpme.org/fs_181

Wortzman, H. (2008, January 9). *Dead sea scrolls.* My Jewish Learning.
https://www.myjewishlearning.com/article/dead-sea-scrolls/

Yahwism. (2023, June 5). Wikipedia.
https://en.wikipedia.org/wiki/Yahwism

Younes, A. (2018, July 19). *Critics call Israel's nation-state law "provocative and racist."* Al Jazeera.

https://www.aljazeera.com/news/2018/7/19/critics-call-israels-nation-state-law-provocative-and-racist

Youssef, H. (2023, October 23). *How the Israel-Hamas war impacts regional relations.* United States Institute of Peace. https://www.usip.org/publications/2023/10/how-israel-hamas-war-impacts-regional-relations

Zacuto, A. ben S., Farissol, A., Moreau, P., Seixas, M., Washington, G., De La Motta, J., Jefferson, T., Worthington, W., Brackenridge, H. M., Maerschalck, F., Myers, M., Karigal, H. I., Blaskowitz, C., Seixas, G. M., Monis, J., Franks, A., Smith, J. R., Carvalho, S. N., Drie, C. N., & Moise, P. (2004, September 9). *Fom haven to home: 350 years of jewish life in america.* Library of Congress. https://www.loc.gov/exhibits/haventohome/haven-haven.html

Zionism. (2024, February 4). Wikipedia. https://en.wikipedia.org/w/index.php?title=Zionism&oldid=1203159685

Image References

Adarrak, A. (n.d.). *Pelayo, king, reconquista image* [Image]. Pixabay. https://pixabay.com/photos/pelayo-king-reconquista-asturias-2160311/

baillif. (2016). *Persepolis Iran ancient Persia* [Image]. Pixabay. https://pixabay.com/photos/persepolis-iran-ancient-persia-1548875/

Black, H. (2018). *Beige concrete buildings on high ground* [Image]. Pexels. https://www.pexels.com/photo/beige-concrete-buildings-on-high-ground-2087392/

bogitw. (2015). *Mosaic, church, wall image.* [Image]. Pixabay. https://pixabay.com/photos/mosaic-church-wall-picture-1009655/

caciaca. (2014). *Alhambra, Granada* [Image]. Pixabay. https://pixabay.com/photos/alhambra-granada-spain-architecture-503208/

Cottonbro Studio. (2020). *Bearded man holding a book* [Image]. Pexels. https://www.pexels.com/photo/bearded-man-holding-a-book-4033827/

Declaire, L. (2016). *Greek writing, engraving* [Image]. Pixabay. https://pixabay.com/photos/greek-writing-engraving-stele-1368146/

eikira. (n.d.). *Hammurabi codex* [Image]. Pixabay. https://pixabay.com/photos/hammurabi-hammurabi-codex-code-1626388/

Geo, A. (2019). *A painting on the ceiling of a building* [Image]. Unsplash. https://unsplash.com/photos/a-painting-on-the-ceiling-of-a-building-1rBg5YSi00c

Giugliano, M. (2022). *Alhambra in Granada* [Image]. Pexels. https://www.pexels.com/photo/alhambra-in-granada-10981668/

hosnysalah. (2018). *Gaza strip Palestine* [Image]. Pixabay. https://pixabay.com/photos/gaza-strip-palestine-3829414/

Mardis, T. (2018). *Hebrew scroll* [Image]. *Unsplash*. https://unsplash.com/photos/white-printer-paper-xUXGHzhIbN4

Ostrower, B. (2018). *A picture of a star of David on a wall* [Image]. Unsplash. https://unsplash.com/photos/a-picture-of-a-star-of-david-on-a-wall-7NOy_3Xzlx4

shpeizer. (2015). *Israel, Zefat, Old image* [Image]. Pixabay. https://pixabay.com/photos/israel-zefat-old-city-galilee-988176/

Smier, S. (2022a). *Be'er sheva, Abraham's well, Solomonic gates image* [Image]. Pexels. https://pixabay.com/photos/beer-sheva-abrahams-well-7478162/

Smier, S. (2022b). *Masada national park* [Image]. Pixabay. https://pixabay.com/photos/masada-national-park-masada-7427144/

Trần, T.-N. (2019). *Close up of the flag of Israel* [Image]. Pexels. https://www.pexels.com/photo/close-up-of-the-flag-of-israel-against-blue-sky-17594309/

Valerich, K. (2018). *Dome of the Al-Aqsa mosque in Jerusalem* [Image]. Pexels. https://www.pexels.com/photo/dome-of-the-al-aqsa-mosque-in-jerusalem-15166635/

Virgilio, M. (2021). *Grayscale photo of man holding sword statue* [Image]. Unsplash. https://unsplash.com/photos/gray-scale-photo-of-man-holding-sword-statue-DvSUgoPoVMQ

Winegeart, K. (2020). *Auschwitz* [Image]. Unsplash. https://unsplash.com/photos/grayscale-photo-of-concrete-bridge-JioCsloIYro